T0072546

Dilkusha by the

Ginkgo Tree

Order this book online at www.trafford.com
or email orders@trafford.com

Most Trafford titles are also available at major online book retailers.

Note for Librarians: A cataloguing record for this book is available from Library
and Archives Canada at www.collectionscanada.ca/amicus/index-e.html

Printed in Victoria, BC, Canada.

ISBN: 978-1-4120-6437-8 (sc)

*Our mission is to efficiently provide the world's finest, most
comprehensive book publishing service, enabling every author to
experience success. To find out how to publish your book, your way, and
have it available worldwide, visit us online at www.trafford.com*

Trafford rev. 2/9/2010

Trafford
PUBLISHING® www.trafford.com

North America & international
toll-free: 1 888 232 4444 (USA & Canada)
phone: 250 383 6864 ♦ fax: 812 355 4082

Contents

Foreword

I was a miner, soldier, sailor, rich man, poor man, teacher. These are my recollections of the end of two empires – the Japanese and the British – of growing up in Korea, America and England, of visits to 40 other lands and of making myself understood in 10 languages.

These are the recollections of the solitary child of the Taylor family, of Seoul, Korea, the heir to a considerable fortune swept away by World War II and the Korean War. Those wars slammed that door shut. "*Muntata!*" as we used to say in Korean. "Shut the door!" And I had to start all over again as a teacher, eventually gaining recognition in the use of the Lozanov Method, resulting in contact with educators all over the world.

One's formative years makes a deep imprint on one's adult life. I am technically an American citizen, from my father. My mother, who was English, acquired American citizenship by marriage but was nevertheless British through and through.

I received a largely British education, so regardless of the countries we lived in, our home was essentially British. However, I lived in Korea from birth to almost 6 years old, learning Korean and English. Over the next four years I learnt Spanish in California at a rather strict Military Academy, then eight years in English schools rewarded me with Latin and French. A return to Korea for three years added Japanese. In California, I studied Chinese. Later, there was exposure to a little German and Italian, further training in Spanish, plus Esperanto.

These linguistic glimpses, education in three continents and travel in the diverse lands of Asia, the Americas, Europe and the South Pacific, has made me feel that I am a World Citizen rather than of any one country.

It is strange how the past catches up with you.

Introduction

Though Korea is geologically a young land, shown by its jagged mountains, its civilization is ancient, stretching back 5,000 years.

Lying between Japan to the east, China to the west and north, and Siberia to the north-east, it extends south toward the Korea Strait, which separates the mainland from Kyushu, the southernmost island of Japan, and the Korean island of Cheju-Do. In the east, short steep rivers plunge into the Sea of Japan from the high, jagged Diamond Mountains, named after the Diamond Sutra of Buddhism. Sweeping west, the land descends to an arable plain – the rice bowl of Korea.

Four westward flowing rivers water this plain: the Yalu on the northern border; the Tai-Tong, which flows through Pyong Yang, the North Korean capital; the Han, which follows a course through Seoul, the South Korean capital, whose port, Inchon, with one of the world's highest tides, makes navigation rather tricky. There is a huge modern airport at Inchon now. To the south lies the Nak-Tong. In the past all these rivers provided power for grinding grain and gold ore.

Having been a vassal state of China for centuries, much of Korea's civilization was derived from its neighbour. In turn, Korea's religious ideas and ideographic writing were passed on to Japan. Yet some of its own ideas were centuries ahead of other countries, including an astronomical observatory built in 634 AD, movable metal type developed two centuries ahead of Europe and armoured warships sent into battle in the 16th century. Rain gauges, sun dials and water clocks were also independently developed. And Hangul, its phonetic alphabet developed in 1440, is said to be one of the world's finest orthographic systems.

Korea excluded foreigners for centuries and became known as the Hermit Kingdom. In 1866 Russia, France and America tried to make contact. Japan succeeded in 1876, then America in 1882, followed by Germany and Great Britain. By 1890 Christian missions from, among others, America, Canada, England and Australia sent missionaries, teachers and doctors, establishing churches, schools and hospitals.

Around this time, the Japanese suggested that Korea's King Kojong be addressed as Emperor. Kojong, known as The Lord of a Thousand Isles (there are in fact more than 3,000 islands off Korea's coasts), proclaimed Korea an empire, giving him a status equal to the Emperor of Japan. Also around this time the American Trading Company sold an electric light plant to the Korean Emperor to illuminate his palace. The Emperor paid in raw gold extracted from his mines.

Together they formed the Oriental Consolidated Mining Company (known as the OCM) in Pyeongonbuk-do, the northern province of Korea, where the Emperor had gold mines. ATC provided mining equipment and brought in experts including my grandfather, George Alexander Taylor, a millwright who built what was then the world's largest stamp mill in Alaska, and my father, Albert Wilder Taylor, a recently graduated mining engineer from the University of California.

Having defeated China towards the end of the 19th century, Japan then overcame Russia in the Russo-Japanese War of 1904-05, with much of the combat taking place in Korea. My father became a war correspondent in those years. Japan immediately started taking control of Korea and in 1910 Korea was declared a Japanese province. At that time its territory stretched from the Yalu river to the Korea Strait, including the island of Cheju-Do. This colonial status lasted until 1945 with the end of World War II.

My grandfather died in 1908, so the next Taylor generations lived mainly under Japanese rule, with Koreans as a subservient race. After many years at the OCM my father became manager of the Chiksan Gold Mining Company, about 60 miles south of Seoul. While in Japan ordering a gold dredge from California he met and fell in love with a beautiful British actress who went by the stage name of Mary Linley. He proposed to her, promising her that when his dredge was running he would go to India, the next stop for her travelling theatrical company, to marry her. In 1917 he did just that – and brought her home to Seoul.

Foreigners in Korea sometimes helped the Koreans' struggle for freedom from Japan. Missionaries brought religion, education and medicine. Businessmen brought Western goods. In January 1918 President Woodrow Wilson spoke of right of self-rule for small nations in a speech to the League of Nations. Korean patriots were inspired. On 1 March 1919, they declared independence from Japan. The American Presbyterian Severance Hospital had a mimeograph machine which had been busy turning out copies of the declaration, distributing them all over Seoul. Japanese police, searching for the source, raided the hospital and brutally crushed the demonstrations.

Two days later, Emperor Kojong, the first emperor of the Korean Empire, was buried. My father was appointed by Associated Press to cover his funeral. The Japanese, with little respect for live Koreans, respected the dead, so it was fitting in their eyes that Koreans should gather in their thousands from all over the country to honour their late emperor.

PART I

1

A New Dawn In Seoul

1 March 1919. Born the day before, I was unaware of the events swirling around me, so it was years before I learned of my father's appointment as special correspondent for the Associated Press to cover King Kojong's funeral.

King Kojong's Funeral Procession in Seoul

When my father came to Severance Hospital to see my mother and I, he picked me up – and found a copy of the Korean Declaration of Independence beneath me. A nurse had thrust it there, a step ahead of the Japanese police, who were seeking the source of literature flooding the city.

Dad left at once and sent his brother, Bill, to Japan to cable the news to America before censorship could be imposed in Japan.

Once Bill was safely off to Japan with a copy of the declaration in the hollowed-out heel of his shoe, my father rounded up an American consular official and H H Underwood, a member of a prominent missionary family, to drive many miles south to Ji Amri to witness and photograph a Japanese Army and police massacre of Koreans demonstrating for their freedom from Japan.

On return, when Dad had word from Bill that the news had been sent to the Associated Press in America, he went to the Japanese Governor-General Hasegawa of Korea with his witnesses and photographs.

Hasegawa claimed ignorance of the massacre. Wielding the power of the Press Dad spread the photos before him and said: "Now you know, and may we say in the paper tomorrow that this was a mistake and won't happen again? Otherwise we will spread this story worldwide – and we have the means to do it.

"Meanwhile we will keep the information in the American consular safe. Any repetition, and the story goes around the world."

The Governor backed down, the killings stopped and the newspaper headline read: "HASEGAWA REGRETS".

The Koreans had intended to announce their declaration to coincide with King Kojong's funeral, but brought it forward, fearing the Japanese would uncover their plans. It took the Japanese rulers completely by surprise. I learned of this decades later, though it remained unknown to writers on the subject and Koreans for years. The accuracy of my mother's words were proven 87 years later by comparison of Severance Hospital records with her autobiography, *Chain of Amber*.

When my mother and I left hospital for home we would have passed many of Seoul's most impressive sights: first the railway station, and, just across the street, Nandaemun, the Great South Gate. Going up the street the Japanese called Nandaimon-dori, we would have passed in the shadows of large commercial buildings, banks, shops, hotels and various Japanese colonial government buildings in European styles. Eventually we would have reached what the foreigners called Legation Street, which was lined with foreign embassies and one of the King's palaces, encircled by a high stone wall. Between this and the British Embassy was a lower wall.

This brings to mind a story in which King Kojong and Queen Min, looking over this wall and seeing people playing tennis, wondered why the players' servants weren't doing this hard work for them!

Continuing our journey, we would have passed through the Great West Gate region, with low, single-storey, open-fronted shops leading to the hill sides, where there stood the small three-roomed Korean houses. Passing these we would finally have reached the enclosed garden of our home.

2

The Little Grey Home In West Gate

It was formerly the home of a *yangban*, an upper class Korean official. It had been converted to Western tastes – the under-floor fireplaces and flues removed and the paper-covered stone and mud floors replaced with polished wood, Western-style fireplaces and stoves. The bathroom was a compromise of local supplies, as native houses of that day had no provision for such things, with a canvas bathtub designed for camping which was hung on the clothes-line to dry after use. Buckets and basins held water for washing and the 'bathroom essential' was a hole in the floor with a suitable container beneath, removable from outside the house.

In contrast, the living room was luxury itself. Glass had replaced the former paper windows, so one could see outside instead of the trickling muted light one got in a pure Korean home. Brass-bound clothes chests called *chongs* had been converted into desks. There were Korean black lacquer palace screens with mother-of-pearl inlays depicting gentlemen walking in gardens, and brass palace candlesticks with movable reflectors shaped like butterfly wings converted to electric lights. On the floor lay tiger-skin rugs, which I loved sliding around on.

I recall long icicles hanging from the eves of the roof in winter when there was snow on the ground.

Unlike either an English or American home today, there were none of the electric or electronic devices which simplify our lives now. We had at least four Korean servants instead. One of these was my *ahma*, or nurse-maid, who carried me around outside in the traditional fashion: on her back in a cloth, like a bed sheet, wrapped around us both.

The servant pool was ruled by the *boy* – an adult man, equivalent to an English butler. In common with many Koreans his name was Kim, so he was known as Kimboy. He had served my father for many years and had once gone with him to inspect a mine up the Yangtze river in China. Kimboy saved Dad's life on that trip. The mine belonged to Thomas Ward, a wealthy English resident of Shanghai, whom the Chinese, in attempting to pronounce his name, called 'Tom Wa'.

During the journey my father was accidentally scratched by his dog. He developed blood poisoning and became delirious. Kimboy, taking the matter into his own hands, engaged two coolies with a carrying chair to carry him over mountain trails to a Scottish missionary doctor. The greater weight of an American over a Chinese was too much for one of the coolies, so he quit, leaving only one man to carry my father on the chair. So Kimboy took over and with the remaining coolie carried Dad to the doctor just in time for him to save Dad's life. For what he had done, Dad promised Kimboy a job for life, but when I was born Kimboy went into business on his own.

Some 30 years later, when my parents and I were living in a hotel apartment in Long Beach, California, I went to the hotel office one evening and was introduced by the desk clerk to an English lady. Dorice Ward turned out to be the widow of Tom Wa's son. I told her she must meet my father, who once inspected a mine in China for her father-in-law. Dorice became a good friend of ours.

Apart from us, there were other little scattered groups of foreigners around Seoul. Various American Christian missionary groups had their own houses built within a walled compound where they could live a more or less Western lifestyle. English church missions tended to use large Korean buildings which were internally adapted to English ways. Most foreign houses tended to have somewhat extensive gardens, encircled by walls to increase security. Then there were the foreign consulates' former legation buildings, built when Korea was independent. Now that Korea has its own government again, they have reverted to their original role.

The Japanese residents were mainly in Tongdaemun, Seoul's Great East Gate region, generally in houses of their own style and ways of life. The exteriors were generally wood and the floors were covered with *tatami* (woven straw mats), requiring shoe removal at the entrance. Heating was far less efficient than the Western or Korean methods, being boxes of sand in which charcoal was burned. Their baths were wooden tubs with built-in stoves: water was poured into the tub, and a lid was put in place; a fire was lit and kept going for about two hours, producing a nice hot bath to soak in after they had washed and rinsed off outside the tub.

Most Koreans lived in three-roomed structures of wood frames, straw roofs, mud and wattle sides, and paper-covered doors and windows to let in a little muted light. They had under-floor heating by the smoke from the low kitchen stoves flowing through stone passages under the floor. Unlike the Japanese, bathrooms were not considered necessary, hence the makeshift conversion in our house.

* * * *

When I was born, Dad was manager of the Chiksan Gold Mining Company, with lode and placer mines. The placer deposits were worked by a gold dredge shipped from California, which Dad had ordered in Japan. Having met my mother on that trip he wanted to show her his latest acquisition. A two-year-old called Beatty went along too.

That two-year-old was me. Dad's Christian name was Albert, but he rarely used it. A Scottish friend had called him Bruce because of Dad's Scottish ancestry. I was christened Bruce, and to prevent confusion my initials B.T.T. were used – spelled and pronounced Beatty.

At Chiksan, junior engineer Beatty was introduced to a cast iron bath tub, also from California, with one part missing – the cross-shaped device which keeps the plug from going down the drain. I made myself rather unpopular by trying to see if the bath plug could be forced further down the plug hole. It could. It went right down! The next morning I saw men digging up the drain pipe outside and wondered what they were doing. They were, of course, retrieving the results of my first engineering activity. Bath plugs were unobtainable in bathless Korea, and had to be ordered from California – 7,000 miles away!

Dividends from shares in this mine enabled the construction of a large house named Dilkusha, encircled by a 12-acre garden overlooking Seoul. The house was stocked with all manner of precious things, including a highly valuable collection of ancient Korean celadon called Koriyaki, which the British Museum had sent a man to Korea to buy. My father refused to sell – he was keeping it for life. Later events, however, proved him wrong.

This mineral wealth also paid for an entirely private school education for me in schools thousands of miles from our home in Korea.

A visit to the machinery of the gold dredge fascinated me – not only the Western machinery, but also, in contrast, a Korean automatic rice mill. Rice, poured into the hollowed end of a vertical tree trunk set low in the ground, was pounded by a wooden hammer attached to horizontal beam, pivoted so that water pouring into the opposite spoon-shaped end tilted it down and emptied it, causing the hammer end to pound the rice. When not in use the spoon end was tied up out of the water stream. At the end of our stay at the mine, we all boarded the train back to Seoul and from there to our home in West Gate.

Transportation in the city was by electric trams (street cars), oxcarts, bicycles, some rickshaws and, occasionally, trucks and cars.

One day the adult members of my family and several friends had a picnic on the river Han with some friends. On return some of them had to take a city tram, as one of the cars had broken down. President Wilson's speech, mentioned in the introduction, was evidently taken at face value by the Koreans, who apparently thought foreign powers would rush to displace the Japanese rule of Korea. When this didn't happen the local populace turned on all foreigners as having betrayed them. A tipsy Korean started a riot on the tram, shouting: "Kill the foreigners! Kill the foreigners who betrayed us!"

It was Kimboy who came to the rescue again, battling some of the aggravators to get the family home safely.

3

Forty Li Of Shining Sands

It was decided that the Taylor family should move to the summer house until the furore died down. This house was just south of Wonsan, in North Korea, on a 12-mile beach known as the Forty Li of Shining Sands. Dad, ever the prospector, had valued the gold content of the sands at a few cents per cubic yard.

Our house was at the southern end of the beach, next to a river flowing into Wonsan Bay. Near us were other business people and the Anglican Bishop's house. Thus our family was, on occasion, afforded spiritual comfort of our own denomination. All the buildings were of American design and wooden construction – raised several feet off the sand – so toddlers like myself could easily walk beneath them.

*A black & white painting of the view from our house of
Wonsan Bay and River*

We acquired water from a pitcher pump attached to a pointed, screened pipe driven into the sand. A good session of pumping yielded plenty of water to carry into the house. The bathroom had slats in the floor, so a basin of water poured over the head disappeared into the sand beneath the house! The other convenience consisted of a sliding metal drawer beneath a seat. Korean coolies removed the contents which were used by local farmers as fertilizer. Lighting was generally by kerosene lamps, though some of the missionaries when on leave in the US brought back Coleman petrol (gasoline) lanterns with fragile mantles which gave brilliant light after a lot of pumping to build up the necessary pressure.

A large number of American missionaries also had their summer houses on the sands. They were located around a large auditorium used for religious and other purposes. Behind the houses, for the length of the inhabited beach, was an extensive pine forest. Behind our house and the forest was a reed-choked backwater of the river, with a few trees here and there. Further back were hills and a range of mountains leading south 50 miles more or less to the famous Diamond Mountains, filled with fantastic Buddhist temples and images, with many associated legends.

The Forty Li extended north of our house to the city of Wonsan (Gensan in Japanese) and seemed to go on forever to the south of us. Of all the world's beaches that I have since seen, never have I seen so many clams, which you could literally dig up with your toes, and which Dad was good at turning into New England clam chowder.

It was also here that I got used to the sea and the idea of swimming as the efficient missionaries anchored a Korean junk offshore for swimmers to dive off. My parents, avid swimmers that they were, arranged a floating baby-sitter, fitting me with a lifebelt attached by a cord to the junk. Getting occasional mouthfuls of sea water, I said it tasted "just like chicken soup". Our Korean cook must have been liberal with the salt!

There was plenty to entertain us during our time here: competitions in swimming and various other activities, religious services for the missionaries, and much else. Most of it was beyond the abilities of mere infants, but there was always something to keep us out of mischief.

I recall conceiving the idea, derived from the clarity of sounds from upstairs to downstairs in the wood framed, uninsulated house, that terrific thunder storms were caused by God moving furniture in Heaven! I also recall the array of saucers and other containers ranged around the floor upstairs to catch the drips through the roof!

Looking out to sea, one could see a host of islands, one of which was what the beach residents called Bamboo Island for its hexagonal basalt columns somewhat resembled bamboo. Only three miles out, it was a favourite place for adults to have evening picnics, but kiddies of my age had to stay ashore and be taken early to bed by their *ahmas.*

I recall one evening, standing on the shore with Kwansi, my *ahma*, watching Dad going through the exasperating business of getting a recalcitrant outboard motor to start. He had Mum and a party of friends to take out to Bamboo Island for an evening picnic – if he could get the motor to start! Electric start and recoil starting handles were unknown in those far off days. Dad just wrapped a knotted cord around the flywheel with the knot in a notch, and pulled. After many repetitions the motor finally barked and, after a few more repetitions, roared to life. Eventually Dad and friends were off and little Beatty was off to bed. More than a dozen years and many thousands of miles of travel had to pass before I too was able to picnic on Bamboo Island.

My maternal grandmother, from England, joined us that summer and while there made some paintings of the islands and coastal scenes, which we still have. One is reproduced in this book.

By summer's end, anti-foreign riots in Seoul were over. Dilkusha was completed, so we returned to the Korean capital. Decades later I learned that Czarist Russia had desired Wonsan, for its ice-free port and suggested division of Korea at the 38th parallel. The Japanese turned them down, and in the Russo-Japanese War defeated the Russians and took all Korea for themselves.

4

Dilkusha By The Ginkgo Tree

Dilkusha, our home on the hill above Seoul, was named after a palace in northern India which Mum saw on her honeymoon. The name means 'Palace of Heart's Delight' in Sanskrit. A giant ginkgo tree, centuries old, stood next to our Dilkusha, in a 12-acre garden surrounding the tree and the house. Just beyond its northern border lay the ancient city wall, ascending the mountain to a rocky peak that we called Pulpit Rock.

On returning to Seoul, we enjoyed Dilkusha's magnificence until shortly before my sixth birthday. From the gate and gate house at the entrance, the driveway swept up to the house in a curve, straightening as it reached the ginkgo tree. A lawn was later added to its right, then a steep rocky hillside, surmounted by a pine tree and the boundary fence beyond. Down the hill from the ginkgo was a well fed by a spring in the rock. Going towards the house at a point where the driveway divided, one part going to the kitchen, the other to the granite front steps one could see the words "DILKUSHA 1923 Psalm 127 V.1" cut into the granite cornerstone. My mother explained the inscription's significance with words from the King James version of the Bible:

Except the Lord build the house, they labour in vain that build it:

Except the Lord keep the city, the watchman waketh but in vain.

Going up the granite steps to the porch of the European-style brick-built house, one walked along a partially enclosed porch, the front of the house on the right and the floor of the second storey porch forming a ceiling above. A waist-high, open-work wall on the left allowed a view of the garden below and the city beyond.

The front door opened into a large hall which, to the right, led to the dining room in the front and behind it the kitchen. The dining room was well-lit with large windows along the side facing the drive and the ginkgo tree. More windows looked out on the part of the side that projected beyond the front porch.

These days it brings to mind breakfast in the autumn. For then the persimmons from their trees in the garden had turned from green to orange and were laid out in rows to ripen on the terrace in front of the second storey living room. They were served as a fruit course at breakfast when they were soft enough to eat. At each place setting, there was a ripe, soft persimmon in a Korean brass bowl, with another brass finger bowl to rinse sticky fingers. When you pulled the stalk off the fruit its little cap came with it, allowing you to scoop out the sweet, soft fruit with a spoon.

Another memory of that room was playing with the Lionel electric train set which my Uncle Bill, Dad's brother, had given me, although at first I was more interested in the elaborate wooden box it came in.

At the end of the hall, double doors led to two bedrooms and a bathroom. In front of these doors, a broad staircase ascended to the living room, while to right at the top of the stairs a duplicate set of doors opened onto two more bedrooms and a bathroom. At the opposite end of the living room was Dad's bedroom and bathroom.

There was quite a spectacular view from the house. In front of the living room was a veranda, which Mum called Tickell Terrace. This was my grandmother's maiden name and my middle name. This terrace greatly enhanced the view of the garden and the city beyond, all the way to the river Han. To the south-east lay the Peking Pass Road and beyond it Kwaniksan, whose last syllable means 'mountain'. The ginkgo tree and the city wall were to the north of the house. Years later, I heard that another staircase had led to a third floor with a family chapel and a private museum for Dad's collection of Korean celadon. I had no idea that part of the house existed at the time.

As our house was in the native area of the city where most houses had only three rooms, the power company charged for the number of light bulbs used – one per room – and turned off the power during the day. We had a meter, but still only had power at night!

Shortly after moving into Dilkusha my father developed a rare tropical disease called sprue, for which the local doctors knew no cure, and advised a return to California to seek more advanced medical help. So leaving my mother, grandmother and I, he sailed to San Francisco to stay across the bay at his family home in Alameda. He sent a cable on arrival, then we heard nothing for a year.

In those days, long distance rapid communication by cable could, surprisingly, be sent in English from Korea, as Morse Code was based on English. Local operators, not knowing English, could recognize individual letters of the alphabet and tap out the code. The system was not without its errors though, as operators confused Alameda with Alabama with such frequency that a number of intermittent cables to Dad never reached him.

After a year with us, Granny decided to return to Grandfather in England and Mum decided we should accompany her as far as San Francisco to find out how Dad was getting on. The dark cloud of Dad's illness led us to a totally new and different way of life in California for four years. And for me, education in a strict private military academy.

5

Eastwards To Gold Mountain

We left Seoul shortly before my sixth birthday, in 1925, taking a train to Busan (Fusan), a steamer to Shimonoseki, in Japan, and then another train to Kobe, where we saw the damage from the 1923 earthquake. We sailed from Yokohama to Honolulu, where we spent a day on Waikiki Beach. At that time there were only two hotels next to that beach. I still recall the palm trees lining the shore, but thought little of the coarse coral sand in contrast to the fine golden sand of Wonsan Beach.

I had won first prize in a fancy dress competition among the passengers on our voyage to Hawaii as a result of being dressed by Mum as a Korean gentleman, wearing an adapted pair of pyjamas. We arrived in San Francisco, California, which in the days of the gold rush was called Gold Mountain by the Chinese coming to work in the mines, as their non-phonetic characters have no way of transliterating foreign names.

On arrival at the dockside in San Francisco I was quite taken aback by the stevedores – I was seeing white men doing manual work for the first time in my life.

"Look at all the white coolies, Mummy!" I shrieked.

Dad met us at the dockside, looking terribly wasted and gaunt. He gave us a tour of his family home on Park Avenue in Alameda. The house was then owned by his sister Olive, and we stayed there for some days with her before finding a small apartment for a while in the town.

Shortly thereafter I was enrolled in the Lona Hazard School in Alameda. Though named after the school's owners, I found it to be very aptly named, for there were decided hazards for those who didn't follow its rules. It was a strict military academy-cum-boarding school. Children who didn't follow the rules were upended and spanked on their bare behinds – I found this out the hard way!

Students spent the entire week at the school, although we were able to go home on weekends, wearing our dark military style hats and dark blue dress uniforms with scarlet lined capes, brass buttons on our jackets and insignia on our caps.

Excellent meals were provided in the main house, with strict instructions that all food placed before you was to be eaten, including liver, which I detested. Children who played with their food were expelled to the back porch to finish their meal standing up. I turned this into an easy way of disposing with the loathed liver. Rover, the owners' dog, was my accomplice and quickly consumed the meat, which was far more to his taste than mine.

Due to Mum's British background, it never really occurred to me that the American aspects of the school told the story of my country. To me it was just yet another country we happened to have visited. It was more academic than the tax supported state (public) schools: we learned the three 'R's very well and a lot more besides, including Spanish, dancing

33

(loved by the girls, loathed by the boys), and close order drill, for the boys, in which we got to use especially large Daisy air rifles, with slings like regular Army Springfield rifles.

Piano lessons were also available if requested by parents. Mine did, but why was piano practice always during breaks between classes? I could think of a number of classes I would have been happy to sacrifice for piano practice, but to lose the sacred rite of a free break was just too much and as a result there was no delight in music for me.

The school deeply impressed on me the ability to really enjoy reading and I recall a large, interesting book that told of the remarkable achievements of American pioneers, engineers and others who had made America the envy of the world. Pictures of giant steam shovels which dug the Panama Canal particularly intrigued me. Little did I know at the time that I would travel through that canal only a short time later.

My parents soon moved to San Francisco's Telegraph Hill, to a small house set in a garden with a partial view of San Francisco Bay. Their next move was to Pierce Street, in the north-western part of the city, to an apartment in the bottom of a large house, with access to its garden. Finally they moved to an apartment in Vallejo Street – a small, gardenless building in which they stayed for the longest time of their four years in San Francisco. The reduction in size of living space prepared me for later life in England, where houses were far smaller than I was used to in Seoul.

Weekends in San Francisco were enlivened by various outings, to Golden Gate Park for a row on the pond, or to the beach or swimming in various public pools. On Sundays we went to the Episcopal Church of the Advent near Van Ness Avenue. I recall one summer going to a church camp in the mountains, possibly the Episcopal Camp (which I believe is still used) near Lake Tahoe, which lies between California and Nevada.

In the 1920s one crossed the San Francisco Bay by steam-powered ferry boats. As a weekly passenger I was fascinated by the giant horizontal single-cylinder steam engines of these ferries. The engine was in the centre of the ship with a car deck on either side of it. There were paddle wheels on the ship's sides. Foot passengers went to the decks above.

During our last summer in California the school rented Castle Hot Springs, a former hotel and summer resort in the mountains of Lake County, a considerable distance to the north of San Francisco. Both parents and children were welcome.

We went by ferry to Sausalito and from there by open-topped bus to Middletown, in Lake County, and then on a seemingly endless winding, unpaved road to the resort. This was in a region of many disused mercury mines, formerly supplying mercury to be used in gold recovery from gold mines. There were also hot springs in the region, a sign of present or past volcanic activity.

While Dad was getting his health back, Mum was attending the California School of Fine Arts in San Francisco, and her theatrical skills were put to good use on this trip. I recall a play about St George and the Dragon in which I auditioned for the parts of St George and the rear-end of a two-boy dragon. In another skit Mum was dressed as an English gentleman remarking on the beautiful sunny weather, when everything went black! The local hotel power plant had failed!

Dad came up for at least one weekend, and on a walk to a disused mine I recall him saying such a site filled him with sadness, for the venture was over for that mine and the miners. By the end of summer, an Army doctor from the Philippines had cured Dad of his illness, my parents were planning to return to their Palace of Heart's Delight, when a cable from Dad's brother Bill in Seoul informed them:

DILKUSHA STRUCK BY LIGHTNING, TOTALLY DESTROYED.

PART II

6

Transportation For Transformation

With no home to take me to, my parents decided to send me to a boarding school in Canada, but an English friend dissuaded them, saying that if I was to be so far from home why not send me to England – to what were then considered the best schools in the world?

So while Dad returned to the family business in Korea with his brother Bill, my mother and I set sail for England a few days before my 10th birthday, in February 1929. A family calamity turned into a source of great good for me, influencing my entire life and finding me my wonderful wife, Joyce Phipps, also born in Asia and educated in England.

We sailed that evening in a British ship, the *MV Lochgoil*, through the Golden Gate with the lights of San Francisco twinkling astern of us, passing Drake's Bay near the entrance to the Gate, where centuries before another British seafarer, Sir Francis Drake, had careened the *Golden Hinde* for the long voyage home. We were heading for that short cut not available to Sir Francis – the Panama Canal, which I had read about at the military academy – across the Pacific Ocean and round the Cape of Good Hope at the southern tip of Africa.

Being the sole child on the 12-passenger vessel, a 10,000-ton freighter, I had the run of the ship and a marvellous opportunity to learn the ways of the sea. All the ship's officers and crew were happy to show me the running of the ship and their part in it.

This knowledge was a great help in the second prep school I attended, St Pirans, whose headmaster was a former Royal Navy commander, and a couple of decades later when I was in the US Active Naval Reserve.

Everyone on board was English, thus providing me with a complete introduction to their mannerisms and language. We sailed down the west coast of North and Central America, standing well out to sea, so saw nothing of the land until the day we came into a bay full of anchored ships awaiting their turn to enter and cross the 50-mile Isthmus of Panama, a whole day's voyage. A pilot guided us through a series of locks which raised our ship to the level of the canal over the mountain chain which had been cut away, allowing ships to cross it. Another set of locks lowered the vessel to sea level on the other side.

Ships travelling slowly are hard to steer, so they were precisely guided into and out of the locks by steel cables attached either side of the bow and stern. These ran to four electric locomotives called mules. As the ship approached a lock, huge steel doors swung open, the cables were attached and the ship was pulled in, the doors closing behind it. Water poured into the lock, raising the ship to the level of the water at the other end of the lock, then the mules pulled the ship up rails and out of the lock. Once the cables were cast off, the ship sailed up the canal under its own power.

I learned while writing this account that a retired British

Naval Commander had found that the Chinese had discovered America 71 years before Columbus and had also connected two rivers in Panama, enabling ships of their day to cross the country.[1]

Before the Americans, the French, who had dug the Suez Canal, attempted a similar venture here in Panama, but were defeated by yellow fever which decimated their workforce. Walter Reed, an American Army doctor, found a cure for yellow fever, enabling the Americans to succeed where the French had failed. I had read about this in my book on American achievements, so it was of great interest to go through this canal.

Once through to the eastern end at the port of Colon, troubles for our Captain Falkner started to mount – as did pleasures for the child passenger. We had to spend a week in Colon for engine repairs, during which time there were daily trips to the municipal swimming pool. When my 10th birthday rolled around, the good Captain launched a motor-driven lifeboat to "test it" and we had a picnic on a cut the French made in their effort to dig the Canal.

Repairs accomplished, we set sail, but a few days later the flywheel on the port diesel engine cracked. We returned to Colon for another week of joy (for me). Off again and a week later the flywheel on the starboard diesel engine cracked – back to Colon for repairs and more swimming! Finally we set sail without further delay, three weeks late, braving a howling gale that strained the lanyard to the compressed air whistle on the funnel, which blew all night. Later, in calmer

---

1   Commander Gavin Menzies, Royal Navy (rtd), *1421: The Year the Chinese Discovered the World* (2002); and *1421: The Year that China discovered America* (2003). See also www.1421.tv

weather, one of the other passengers made a kite for me, which we flew off the stern.

During the trip I had a grand tour of the ship, going from the bridge (the control room) to the engine room and on to the wireless room, which started an almost life-long fascination with the wonders of wireless until computers came into my life about 60 years later.

When passing through the Sargasso Sea crew members caught the seaweed in the area complete with tiny crabs crawling on it and bottled it for me.

As we approached England our port of call was changed from London to Liverpool, so we went north past the Bristol Channel towards the Irish Sea when some passenger called out: "Whales! Whales!" We looked all over the place and could see none. Oh yes, there was some land over there, and that was Wales – a principality, not a group of sea mammals!

On arrival at Liverpool, the shipping line gave us first class train tickets to London, where a taxi took us to my grandfather's house in Barnes, a suburb of London on the Thames. By chance the famous annual Oxford and Cambridge Boat Race was in progress on the river in front of the house at the time.

My entire life until then had been one of a local English environment set against an outer alien one, first in Korea, then America. I had at last come to a completely English environment with Grandmother, a delightful lady, whom I had known in Korea, and Grandad, a retired doctor and a very kindly gentleman called Dr Charles Forbes Mouat-Biggs. What a wonderful doctor he must have been! He had been a soldier in South Africa, the personal physician to the Maharajah of Patiala in India, and a British Army doctor in World War I, decorated by the King of Belgium for saving hundreds of men's lives.

He and a family friend, Vivian Rogers, then the Lord Mayor of Westminster, introduced Mum to a suitable tutor to prepare me to enter Vivian's son's prep school in Sussex. The tutor taught me Latin, French and the curious British duo-decimal monetary system. I was accustomed to the decimal systems of Korea and America, so British coinage was very confusing at first, but years later the experience proved useful a second time when I was stationed in Australia with the US Army.

Next we went to Maidenhead, in Berkshire, to meet Mum's brother and his wife, Mr and Mrs Mouat-Biggs – known to me as Uncle Ron and Aunt Mary. Being childless, they agreed to be my guardians. Their home, named *The Cabin*, was on Ray Mill Road near the edge of the town. Uncle Ron, who was in charge of maintenance for a local bus company, was to influence the entire course of my life. Noting his kindly manner I asked him why of all the English coins, only one, the threepenny bit, was hexagonal rather than circular? His reply was that it required a wrench to get it out of a Scotsman's pocket!

7

The English Transformation

Before Mum left to join Dad in Korea, we enjoyed a farewell holiday together in Norfolk. More than five years passed before we met again.

I was left to adapt to the strict, confining way of life provided by the English preparatory and public school system, initially at Thrings Brunswick in Haywards Heath, right out in the West Sussex countryside. I found that preparatory and public schools were elementary and secondary fee-supported private schools, largely formed from the desires of the recently rich middle classes, born of the industrial revolution, wanting their sons to be trained to the level of the ruling classes.

The pattern was set by Dr Arnold, headmaster of Rugby School in 1826, where the game of the same name was first played. He aimed to raise Christian gentlemen rather than mere scholars and the school chapel was central to what was taught. What a contrast to the non-religious schools of America from which I had come. I found that the schools derived from his ideas were of two types: the older, traditional, very strict ones, which I have called the 'driver' type, or the newer 'encourager' kind.

I sampled both and found the latter produced far better results. However, both types required instant inflexible following of rules. Thrings was of the 'driver' type, making no attempt to explain their rules to a new boy, so I floundered around, finding it all very confusing and confining.

The school's grounds belonged to a large country house with a separate chapel, extensive playing fields and lots of room for running and jumping on sports day. It also had an outdoor swimming pool.

Morning Prayer, in the chapel, opened the school day. In addition there were two services on Sundays – Morning Prayer and Evensong. The syllabus included considerably more subjects than my American school, including Latin, French, English history and world geography.

Pupils who had parents or relatives nearby could be taken out on up to three Sundays each term between the two chapel services. Otherwise the only times students left the school grounds were on the Sunday walks around the countryside in crocodile formation, walking in pairs behind each other, with a master in charge.

After the weekend freedom in California I found this very restrictive, as though I was 'doing time' at Thrings for a couple of terms. The whole experience was something of a blur and I longed to get out.

Then suddenly, liberation! A Maidenhead prep school, St Pirans-on-the-Hill, which still exists today, hired a bus from Uncle Ron's company. He saw it as a gem of a school and arranged a transfer with my parents' consent.

This was an 'encourager' school and it transformed the entire course of my life. I learned to love my mother's land, and felt it to be my own. So, at maturity, I sought an English wife. St Pirans was in a pleasant location high above the town of Maidenhead in Berkshire. The school was named after an Irish saint who built his church on the sands of what is now Perrenporth, Cornwall.

Hedges, trees, flowerbeds and extensive green playing fields surrounded our educational home, which always had a friendly feel. I recall no time out with relatives, but there were sports and prize-giving days when many parents descended on the school.

Commander Tippet, a retired Royal Navy officer, was the headmaster – a kindly but strict gentleman with a wealth of knowledge. We addressed him, and all teachers, as 'Sir'. But between ourselves we referred to him as 'Com T' and his motherly wife as 'Ma T'. Most of the other teachers were former British Army officers used to instant obedience.

My two favourite teachers, Commander Tippet and Mr Higgins, a former Army Captain, were both kind but strict. In fact, the whole staff was a kindly lot, interested in their students, encouraging positive efforts, patiently helping the bewildered and generally making the subjects they taught interesting to us.

BUT you jolly well did what you were told, NOW! No backchat! Or else a trip to the headmaster's study to await instant learning in the form of six of the best on the posterior applied with a cane. A great diversity of information and principles were instilled at that school and to this day I am grateful to St Pirans and the wonderful people who ran it. The school had high expectations of learning, fair play, personal standards based on Christian principles and learning to be honest gentlemen. Religion underpinned all other learning – it was how we shaped our lives.

The school motto was 'Live Honourably, Live Strenuously.' I have the school shield with those words and a dragon rampant on it before me as I write.

St Piran's was superbly equipped, even better than many secondary schools. The school grounds were bounded by a tall hedge next to the main road, from which a long drive extended, bordered by horse chestnut trees with cricket fields to one side and a tall hedge on the other. About 100 yards down, the drive was divided at the corner by the chemistry laboratory. One road going to the left divided the school buildings from the cricket grounds. The other went straight ahead then looped back to the headmaster's house and then to the main school entrance. This entrance opened into a hall with most doors on the right being off limits to boys, as they led to the headmaster's quarters, the kitchen, the matron's room and the school dispensary.

Here, some luckless lads had cod liver oil prescribed for their health. Ugh! Lucky ones had the medicine combined with malt, which was an entirely different, delicious concoction. The recipients of this ambrosia had a theory – that if one teaspoonful was good for you, two tablespoons would be better! Our righteousness in taking our medicines was somewhat variable, hence the need for the matron to dispense the doses.

Left of the dispensary, stairs ascended to the headmaster's study where rule breakers awaited their fate. Beyond and above were the boys' dormitories.

Next to the foot of these stairs ran the main passageway

through the building. To the left of the main entrance was the door to 'big school', a large well-lit classroom with a raised platform at the far end and windows on two sides.

Recalling this room, the main classroom for my form, brings back vivid memories of the various subjects we were taught. Geometry by Com T, arithmetic and algebra with Mr Higgins, whose methods I used when I became a teacher. I loved those subjects at St Pirans and did well in them. Other teachers taught us chemistry, English grammar, spelling, writing, reading, literature, English history, world geography, singing, religion, scripture, Latin and French, with practical carpentry and machine shop classes also included in the curriculum.

In contrast with my success in Korean and later in Japanese and Chinese, I struggled with the two languages offered at St Pirans. However, prior to a trip to Paris 40 years later I learned more useful French in three weeks using a form of the Losanov Method called Accelerated Learning.

Once a week Com T convened a group in his study, where he told us all sorts of intriguing things about the world and his adventures in the Royal Navy. His study looked out on to the cricket fields, but at a safe distance so boys hitting cricket balls had no hope of breaking his window. Yet he used say that he would award extra runs to any boy who could break his window during a match! No one ever succeeded while I was there. Among the immutable laws of St Pirans, tree climbing was forbidden, although there was one tree in his garden on which Com T openly encouraged climbing – it was a monkey puzzle tree which had long spikes for leaves! None of the resident monkeys ever took up his offer.

Next along the corridor was the dining hall, which could be

transformed into a theatre by a portable stage. The regular entrance was used by the players behind the stage curtain while the audience used the back entrance. I attained theatrical advancement in this room, stepping up from the rear end of a two-boy dragon in California to a butler in England.

Continuing along the main passage another corridor to the left led to the back entrance of the dining room and a door to one of the classrooms that looked out on the cricket field. All classrooms were equipped with special glass to allow in the sun's healthy rays. How concepts change – now we are urged to use skin cream to ward off those rays!

Between the dining room and classroom doors were stairs, enabling one to ascend on high for spiritual comfort in the chapel. Just past this left-hand passage was one on the right to a locker-lined changing room with rows of wash basins. The entrance to the indoor school pool was in the far corner of that room.

The next room up the main passage on the right side would be called a rest room in America, but we called it the bogs. Then on the left was the classroom exit and the library entrance. Here was a source of many adventure tales for me. On the right, stairs ascended to another classroom and the music rooms. A door at the end of the passage led to a covered breezeway, beyond which was the machine shop and the photographic darkroom. The school was still lit by gas, so a Tangye hot bulb ignition gas engine drove the lathes. Several decades later I saw an identical engine in a museum in Matakohe on North Island, New Zealand, and I also recall seeing them advertised outside Paddington railway station in London, when taking the train to school.

One day during a machine shop class the retaining pin holding one of the engine's two flywheels dropped out, the wheel shot off, smashed against the guard rail, an iron fragment of it cut the shop teacher on the head and wrecked the engine.

In the darkroom, photographers apparently used sunlight to print their negatives. Beyond this building was the gymnasium and outside it were gardens for members of the Gardening Club. I had a plot and devised a centrally arranged system to water radishes, cress, lettuce and other crops, eating them at tea when consumption of one's produce was permitted. To the left of the gardens was the carpentry shop cum rifle range, where I learnt to make various items. The cricket fields were in front of this workshop. Going back past the garden plots the path led to the rugby fields. I enjoyed the constant action of rugby and played in a team years later at College of Marin in California.

In the summer term the school cricket team played against other school teams on Saturday afternoons, with tea and cakes between innings a particularly enjoyable feature.

At certain times there would be a sports day, involving all manner of races. The three-legged race, in which two boys ran side by side with their legs in the middle tied together, and the egg and spoon race were always a source of much merriment. In the latter, runners held a spoon with a hard boiled egg in it and ran, stopping to retrieve it, each time they dropped it. Of course this was constant, causing much amusement to the spectators.

Rugby was the winter sport and as with cricket then our school team played against other schools. No cakes though. Instead, at half time, orange and lemon quarters were passed around to be sucked in lieu of drinks. Following the game all the players and staff had a grand tea in our dining hall.

Aside from classes and sports, outside lecturers occasionally gave interesting illustrated talks. I recall a fascinating talk by a former Navy diver who had aided in raising ships of the former German High Seas Fleet. He showed us slides of the salvage work and his equipment in the school pool. At the end of World War I the Germans had to surrender their fleet to the Royal Navy, but when they reached the huge harbour of Scapa Flow in the Orkney Islands, they scuttled their ships rather then turn them over to the victorious British. For me at least, this turned out to be a two part lesson. The second part, 70 years later, was when my wife, Joyce, and I went to Scapa Flow in 2001! Such experiences at school expanded our interests and stimulated our desire to learn more.

On Guy Fawkes Day, 5 November, we had a terrific fireworks display on the cricket fields provided by a parent who owned a fireworks factory. We would chant: "Remember, remember the 5th of November. Gunpowder, treason and plot."

Guy Fawkes had been caught trying to blow up the Houses of Parliament in the 17th century. Every year since then there is a celebration that his plot was foiled. Over 40 years after leaving St Pirans this date became personally important to me as it was the day on which my remarkable mother passed from this life. Her autobiography, *Chain of Amber*, illustrates her adventurous life, mostly in Korea. Years later it led most of our family back to Korea.

Returning to our life in St Pirans, our daily schedule began at 6.30am on weekdays, dressed in running gear with Com T leading around the extensive school boundaries, an exercise we called 'beat the bounds'. On return, we washed and changed into our school uniforms of grey shorts and woollen stockings, black leather shoes, grey jackets and waistcoats and our St Pirans ties of diagonal light blue, dark blue and yellow stripes. Then breakfast and a break followed by ascension to the school chapel for morning prayer.

Morning classes followed, then mid-morning break and more classes, then lunch. After a free period in winter, we played rugby, having tea and biscuits before more classes. Summer afternoon classes were followed by the sedate game of cricket. Rounders, a lively game rather like baseball, but played with a soft rubber ball, was occasionally substituted, which pleased me as I found rounders more interesting. At the end of the day we had supper, called 'big tea' – the previous snack being 'little tea'. We preceeded that with another free period, homework, evening prayers and then bed, where often a kindly master read a story to us. Once the gas lights were turned down and out the master would order: "SILENCE!"

On Sundays we were up at about 7am. We washed, dressed and had some free time before and after breakfast before Holy Scripture class from the King James Version of the Bible, reinforcing our detailed instruction in daily Bible lessons in the chapel services. The lessons exposed us to the lovely language of the King James translation, shaping our use of English in the years to come. Later that morning, we ascended on high to attend Divine Worship.

A nice little touch of Com T's was to record the entrance and leaving dates together with the pupils' names on the chapel walls so they would be remembered before God. Returning to St Pirans many years later I was touched to find my name there.

After chapel, boys with overseas parents, such as myself, went to the headmaster's dining room under Ma T's instruction and wrote letters to our distant parents. Lunch was next, followed by some free time. After this we walked in pairs to some distant point under the guidance of a master.

On return we had some free time, then little tea, Evensong, big tea, free time, bed and the usual stories.

Rules were rigid at St Pirans, and the dining room was no exception. All food placed before you was to be eaten and none removed from the room. On Fridays we had fish – *a whole fish*! I had not the slightest idea of what to do with it! Fish was always filleted in my American school. The other boys, by some kind of magic, knew how to get the meat off this barbed wire fence. I temporarily solved the problem by putting the mangled fish in a handy drawer and for a long time decided I didn't like fish.

I circumvented the dining rules on another occasion, bringing a box camera in with me, having removed its film carrier to stow three slices of bread in its place. After supper, with two companions, I toasted the contents before the chemistry lab fire and consumed the evidence before a master came in to tell us not to burn paper in the grate! The three little sinners assured him they wouldn't.

At the end of term, parents arrived – usually in expensive vehicles like Jaguars and Bentleys – to return their sons to their estates for the holidays. Uncle Ron arrived in his blue, two-seater Rover with folding roof and rumble seat, which opened up to reveal an open-air seat in the curved trunk at the back. He turned the corner, stopped just beyond the chemistry lab, where I was awaiting him, and whisked me and my luggage down the hill to his home.

8

My English Home

As we went in Uncle Ron's car my thoughts fled across the seas and continents to the distant land of sharp-peaked mountains and white-clothed people, oxcarts plodding along the side of the road, men carrying great loads on their backs, bicycles here and there and cars dodging around them; the people speaking an ancient tongue which I once spoke, Korean, in addition to my parents' English.

My thoughts ascended the mountain to the Palace of Heart's Delight overlooking the walled city of my birth. This was my true home, with its ancient, giant ginkgo tree, persimmon and Siberian cherry orchards and other bushes and trees. Here my wonderful English mother lived in the company of my remarkable American father, with servants in the house to do their every bidding.

Returning to the present, Uncle Ron stopped outside his home, The Cabin. The house was named in the English manner rather than numbered in the American, or for that matter the Japanese and Korean way, of numbering houses in the order they were built. This little home had none of the views, location or size of Dilkusha, and no servants to assist in its upkeep.

Uncle Ron had once lived in a palatial home, also staffed with servants, but World War I ended that life. He learned too late in life that he could have had Scottish training as a doctor, following in his father's footsteps, so he had resorted to his automotive hobby to become manager of maintenance for the local bus company.

He married Mary Craske, a nurse who had taken care him while recovering from war wounds. She was of Polish origin but had lived in Eastbourne, East Sussex, on England's south coast, and had converted to British life to the extent that she was more British than some of the British! By careful use of Ron's salary and his mechanical skills, the couple were able to maintain a car and a nice little home to live a life in which next to nothing was ever thrown away – there was always some use for most things.

In my own adult married life, that 'pack rat' tendency has been a source of exasperation to my darling wife Joyce. There is hardly a thing that she tosses out that I don't pounce on and find a use for!

Returning to my boyhood, there were two groups of semi-detached, brick-built houses on Uncle Ron's quiet road, near the junction of another road. At this point I discovered a wonderful device, unknown in Korea at that time, which enabled amazingly speedy contact with my distant parents on the other side of the globe. It was the red Royal Mail post box: letters posted there could be sent across the world and – if I was very lucky – I might get a reply in only one month!

Every day I would walk with Uncle Ron along the tree-lined Ray Mill Road. At places along this road were some comparatively large houses, and groups of cottages at another point, then open fields, a modern housing estate and two sizeable single house estates next to Boulter's Lock, on the river Thames. On one of them was a sign: "Beware of the dog!"

Some wit, noticing the lack of barking, had written in chalk: "Ware be the dog?"

While waiting by the lock for the bus to High Wycombe, where Uncle Ron worked, we would watch the boats slowly rise as the water flowed in when its gates were shut. Beyond the lock keeper's house was the old mill which gave our road its name.

On returning home, I would walk with Aunt Mary across nearby fields to the High Street shops. First we stopped at Eve the Butcher, where meat items were displayed on marble slabs open to the street. Next, passing the Westminster Bank, we entered the International (Grocery) Stores where each department had its own clerk who handed you your items. You took everything to a central clerk who added your purchases and collected your money. When all was complete, we returned home, Aunt Mary carrying her laden basket – everything but milk and bread, which were delivered to the door by the dairyman and baker's man.

The front garden of The Cabin had a low brick wall with a cast iron fence and a hedge inside it, beyond which were flower beds and two paths, one leading straight to the recessed front door and the other curving around to the side and back. If one entered the house through the front door, which we rarely did, on the right was the drawing room for entertaining occasional visitors. Here were mementoes inherited from past generations and gifts from my family in Korea, including brass shoes made for use as ashtrays and an infant photo of myself on a tiger skin, taken in the living room of the Little Grey Home in the West, in Seoul. Beside an assortment of chairs and a couch, there were some antique glass-fronted cupboards of French origin, from Louis XIV's era, brought from my grandmother's home in Cheltenham.

In the passage outside this room, stairs ascended to the bathroom and bedrooms. Beside the stairs another door opened into the dining room with French doors leading to the back garden. This room was in daily use as a living room and only rarely for guests as a dining room. On those occasions a little opening cut through the wall was used to pass food directly from the kitchen. This was one of the many improvements made by my ingenious Uncle Ron. In here also was the family wireless (radio), which was replaced by a television set many years after I had left. The kitchen was more handy for our daily meals. To the left of its entrance door from the passage was a black painted wall, where once a coal-fired cooking stove sat, but had been replaced by a table where we ate our meals. Beyond it were various cupboards and in front of the opposite wall was the gas stove and oven. A geyser – a gas-fired water heater – supplied hot water to the kitchen sink. The back door, next to the sink, led to a concrete area which was met by the path that led around the side of the house.

The lawn came to the edge of the concrete where there was a bird-feeder mounted on a pole with a house-like roof over it. We called it Dilkusha – after my distant home. There was also a coal shed in the garden, and a large garden-shed-cum-workshop which housed a bicycle, tools and a work bench. The lawn, with flower beds around its edges, continued to the end of the garden where a cherry tree grew. When I lived in America I had heard a somewhat fictional tale of George Washington and a cherry tree. Well, here is my own cherry tree tale.

One afternoon I mounted the cherry tree to sling an aerial from it to my room after Aunt Mary's nephew, Robbie, had built me a one-valve battery-powered wireless set. I presumed Aunt Mary approved, as she didn't come out to stop me. However, she was taking a nap at the time and certainly did not approve, but she didn't want me risking my neck a second time so the aerial stayed!

Later in Korea I used my scant radio knowledge to circumvent the Japanese censorship, enabling us to get foreign newscasts. Later still, I became a US Army radio operator. In retirement I considered getting an amateur radio license, but found that computers gave more reliable long distance contact, so switched to them, and now have computer friends around the world.

My room in The Cabin, at the top of the stairs, had the skull of a boar with a hole in its head mounted on the wall opposite my bed. Grandfather had shot it with a revolver when it charged him in an Indian jungle. On the other wall was a map of the world with a finger of land coming down from Manchuria and Russia between Japan and China, my distant birthplace, Korea.

Beyond my room was the bathroom, complete with another gas-fired geyser to provide hot baths. Turning left and up a short flight of stairs one came to a spare bedroom with a window looking down on the back garden. On the landing just outside the spare and master bedrooms at the front of the house was a chest of drawers surmounted with a silver model of a small pony trap carriage – a wedding gift for my grandmother, Uncle Ron's mother, from her Irish tenants. Next to it was a photo of the vehicle complete with pony.

Sixty-nine years later in Baltinglass, County Wicklow,

Ireland, my wife and I saw the land where my grandmother had once lived and, at the parish church, the memorial those same tenants had put up in honour of her father, Commander Thomas Tickell RN, whom they greatly appreciated. Some years after my grandmother's marriage to Dr Charles Forbes Mouat-Biggs, the couple bought a large house in Cheltenham, where their children were raised. World War I ended that standard of living and the house became a hotel, then an office building, such was its size.

For eight years, my childless uncle and aunt experienced the joys of raising a child, living in a little house of the lower middle class, never thinking that I was going to schools of the very wealthy. I didn't conceive at that time that my parents' standard of living in Korea was that of American millionaires. The size of our home in Seoul was only exceeded by some Embassy and Consular houses, or the Japanese Governor-General's mansion.

I was due to inherit Dilkusha, along with our office building in Seoul, our summer house in North Korea and the family gold mine further south in the same region. However, World War II and the Korean War swept it all away, and I, like my Uncle Ron, had to start all over again. Sometimes in my little room at The Cabin I would ponder over the world map on the wall, look again at north east Korea and go back in my mind to The Haven, our summer home on The Forty Li of Shining Sands in North Korea.

I went on real little excursions from time to time with my aunt and uncle, such as blackberry picking or mushroom gathering in the fields. One Christmas they gave me Uncle Ron's bicycle and once I had learned to ride it I visited all the nearby towns and villages such as High Wycombe, Bray, Furze Platt, Maidenhead Thicket and Cookham.

For several years we spent Uncle Ron's annual holidays in Cornwall with the Crossley-Meates family – boyhood friends of Uncle Ron and my mother, and also mine, as I went to St Pirans with Roy Crossley-Meates. Their house was on a valley side, leading down to Gillan Cove at the mouth of the Helford river, south of Falmouth. We went around with the Crossley-Meates in their boats and cars and saw some fascinating sights, including a short flight over St Michael's Mount in a open cockpit two-seater biplane. A great thrill in those far-off days!

The rocky Cornish coast was something of a graveyard for ships, being on the main shipping lane to several of England's major ports. Not far from the Lizard Head Lighthouse, several miles south of the Helford river mouth, were three wrecked submarines which on the way to a scrap yard – they were scrapped on the rocks before they got there!

At times Stella, Roy's sister and I, would borrow a family rowing boat and row up the bay extending from Gillan Cove to see small shrubs only a couple of feet high bearing what appeared to be tiny plums. They were, in fact, blackthorn bushes bearing sloes, which have a sharp, sour taste and are used to flavour gin.

Among Uncle Ron's other expeditions from Maidenhead were trips to Olympia, a big exhibition hall in London, to see science showcases. I recall seeing an early television set, made before the TV tube had been invented in America. It was like looking into a rapidly turning wheel with a somewhat indistinct image in it. Sometimes we drove to Whipsnade Zoo, near Luton, in Bedfordshire, and spent the day there. It had fields for animals instead of cages – much nearer to their natural habitat.

As I grew towards driving age Uncle Ron taught me to drive, and shortly before I left England I took a commercial driving course, although it was not until after World War II that I drove again, as the roads of Korea left a lot to be desired.

9

Public Schools

Eventually the time came, in 1933, when I had to leave
St Pirans and attend a public school (private high school).
My parents' preferred option was Brighton College, in the
town of that name in Sussex, on the English Channel coast.
Brighton and Hove form a dual seaside resort, and on the
eastern side is an area called Kemptown, where Brighton
College still flourishes.

I was most fortunate to be assigned to Walpole House, the
only one off the school grounds, which in contrast to the rest
of the school was of the 'encourager' type. The housemaster
and his wife, Mr and Mrs George Shallow, delightful
people with positive attitudes, provided food and lodging
of a superior order. All the other houses, which were of the
older, stricter 'driver' type, were on the school grounds along
with the chapel and classrooms, swimming pool, machine
shop, carpentry shop, auditorium and cricket field/parade
ground. These were within a block encircled by a fence of
cast iron posts, inside of which were grassy banks bedecked
with trees. A road encircled the fence, beyond which were
rows of houses.

On arising in the morning you had the choice of starting the
school day with a cold bath in an unheated bathroom, or an
equally cold shower, "to toughen you up". I chose a shower
because I could get out of it faster! After dressing and roll-

call, we had breakfast, then off to school. Morning Prayer in the school chapel started the day.

One went to different classrooms for various subjects. Unlike at St Pirans, the teaching style was transfer of information – and if you didn't get it, you were stupid. No checking to find out why you didn't understand. Maths was my favourite subject at St Pirans, but I failed dismally at Brighton, as neither I nor the teacher realised that I was really in need of glasses. The teacher thought I was stupid and I concluded I couldn't learn maths.

Years later, I found that eyesight is apt to change at puberty; mine did, for the worse, and mathematical signs got mixed up. The English composition teacher paid me an unintentional compliment, for when I turned in a carefully worded and erudite essay on my hobby of geology I was given a score of 3/10 for good writing. He thought I had copied the article from an encyclopedia! At that time I was an avid reader of geological material and spent much of my holidays in the Geological Museum in South Kensington, London.

However, good came of it years later when I became a teacher in California: I always sought the reason why children failed and tried positive ways to encourage them, and quite number of times I had the great joy of turning supposed failures into academic successes.

Outside academia I was thrust into Brighton College's choir and Officers' Training Corps, although I only lasted a year in the choir before my voice broke. The OTC, on the other hand, swept everyone up – even a stray American!

Physical education was conducted for the most part on the Brighton Race Course, to which we walked the mile or so every day. Curiously, about three decades later in Santa Rosa, California, I met an English car salesman who also used the race course during his time at a Christian Brother's School in Brighton.

Other non-curricular activities included machine shop and wood shop. We had somewhat more freedom than in my previous schools, being allowed down town for an hour and a half on Wednesdays, two and half hours on Saturdays, and to walk along the sea front for an hour on Sunday mornings after Chapel. On Sunday afternoons we had a walk to a point where roll would be checked before returning to the House. Now and then everyone in Walpole House would go down to the beach and swim in the sea. Part of my first year there was the last for a popular headmaster, Canon Dawson, a Church of England priest. As he left, so did a considerable number of students.

A year of falling enrollment after his retirement caused the school to close Walpole House at the end of the next year. Boys would be transferred to the older houses on the school grounds – not a happy prospect for us. But, to our joy, we learned that our Mr. Shallow was to become headmaster of All Hallows, an ancient, smaller public school in Honiton, Devon. We were invited to go with him and form a new Walpole House. As the fees were less, many of our parents, including mine, were delighted – and so were their sons – thus the transfer was made.

* * * *

Devon! Sir Francis Drake, England's great globe-encircling naval hero, was a Devon lad. For a time we too would enjoy education in 'Glorious Devon' as the railway advertising of the time called it. Better still, with George Shallow at the helm, All Hallows proved to be another 'encourager' school, which further advanced my love of my ancestral land. So the next term I took the rail route of the Cornish Riviera Express a hundred or so miles further to school in the little old country town of Honiton, dating back beyond Roman times, set in a lovely valley of trees and green fields, with a river running by. An Iron Age fort overlooked the valley from a hill to the north. Honiton's High Street ran straight through the centre of town, with shops and houses on either side.

Near the town centre was St Paul's Parish Church and beside it a chapel for its choir school, All Hallows. The chapel was built in the 12th century and since then had been to a grammar school, preparatory school and finally a public school. Nearby was the Town Hall and then the street proceeded down hill to what was left of the Roman road, then onward to the city of Exeter, about 13 miles to the west.

Over 60 years later I found that not only had Sir Francis Drake once owned land a few miles north of Honiton, where All Hallows had been in existence for centuries before his time, but one of his descendents still lived nearby. And at that time, as a member of the Drake Navigator's Guild, I was able to send him a book which told of Sir Francis's adventures on the other side of the world in Drakes Bay, just north of the entrance to San Francisco Bay,in Point Reyes National Sea Shore,in Marin County, California.

Things at All Hallows contrasted starkly to Brighton College. The school, its town and the countryside all had such a friendly feel. We had far more liberty here than in the other English schools that I had attended. This was a region of ancient historical and geological interest. George

Shallow gave me free reign in the chemistry lab to conduct tests on mineral samples that Dad had sent from our family gold mine in North Korea.

Back to Honiton. The grounds of the school were rather scattered around the town. Evidently, the school acquired what land it could find as it expanded over the centuries. The main buildings were next to St Paul's Parish Church, the chapel and the attached dining hall forming an L-shaped building there. Another building was attached, containing the kitchen, some of the dormitories and a sick room.

Rooms behind St Paul's included a good-sized theatre and a room where morning roll-call and evening homework were conducted. Tradition required that one answered the roll-call with the Latin "Adsum." ("I am here.") If our pals were late we would say "Absum-t!" as the English 'absent' was used to indicate missing persons.

The main school area was reached by a footbridge over Silver Street, which divided the church land from the school land behind it. The land beyond the bridge contained most of our classrooms, the gymnasium, a playground/OTC parade ground, plus rifle range backed up by a thick sturdy stone wall of old red Devonian sandstone, encircling the cattle market next door. A little further on were the school carpentry shops, beyond which the land sloped down to the River Gissage. The wall curving around the cattle market led to the school's outdoor swimming pool, then to a tree-lined lane leading to the river. Beyond the lane was an extensive cricket ground and pavilion for use during inter-school cricket matches.

Returning to the High Street, at least one more classroom could be found by crossing the road and walking down a driveway next to Dimond's Book Shop. I recall studying Shakespeare's *Julius Caesar* there and the master declaiming: "You blocks, you stones, you worse than senseless things! You hard hearts, you cruel men of Rome, knew you not Pompey? Many a time and oft have you climb'd up to walls and battlements, to towers and windows, yea, to chimney-tops, your infants in your arms, and there have sat the livelong day, with patient expectation, to see the Great Pompey pass the streets of Rome."

Blocks and stones? I think he was playfully referring to us!

Behind this building were dormitories which backed on to a kitchen garden wall, handy for night time escapades by certain characters in our midst who would walk along the top of the thick brick wall from the dorm to the local back street fish and chip shop! Across from the dormitories were bathrooms, behind the bookshop. I distinctly recall picking up an odd piece of lead water pipe which I later melted down to cast a lead duplicate of an ammonite fossil to use as a paper weight.

After the first term, during which the Brighton College transferees stayed in this building, we were moved, as promised, to our own Walpole House up the hill beyond Honiton railway station. It was one of those semi-detached houses so common in England. We had our own kitchen, but as all meals for the whole school were served in the main dining hall next to our chapel, it remained unused, enabling junior metal-casting activities by an intended future mining engineer.

Due to our greater liberty, I became acquainted with much of the surrounding countryside as well as their fossils and rocks. I distinctly recall walking beside the Gissade, which ran through the valley below Honiton, and picking up a rather poor fossil of a shell, but on turning it over found an almost perfect impression of a fish's tail showing the scales as well. The gravel shores of this river produced quite a few fossils which eventually joined a college display in Korea.

The countryside provided such a wealth of experience: on Sunday afternoons we would go for long walks, on other occasions we would have cross-country runs and sometimes we would follow the local Beagle hounds chasing rabbits. It was a lovely country existence, far more to my liking than the over-crowded streets of Brighton. Many people think of Brighton as the ideal seaside resort, but to me it was a last resort!

Towards the end of my last summer term in 1936, Mum came from Korea to see me at school and on meeting George Shallow pointed out that in the event of war I would be in the American Army. On Fridays, OTC parade days, the bridge behind the parish church often derived me of my leggings wrapped like bandages around our legs. I just couldn't get the hang of how to make them stay on and they often unravelled on my 'bridge of despair', so I was doubly delighted when released from further OTC training!

Mum's words proved prophetic, for about five years later, on 7 December 1941 the Japanese attacked Pearl Harbour. I was a soldier in the US Regular Army at Schofield Barracks, 30 miles to the north. On the same day both my parents and my future parents-in-law, the British Consul-General and his wife, were interned in Seoul by the Japanese Police as enemy aliens.

During Mum's visit George Shallow gave me extended leave to have whole weekends away from school to be with her. We used my copy of *Stanford's Geological Atlas of Britain* to choose places to visit. We would find deposits of small ammonites in a bank near Frome, in Somerset, and a great diversity of ammonites and belemnites on the beach at Lyme Regis, Dorset, including one ammonite about a foot in diameter which I lugged back to the railway station and eventually got to The Cabin's garden where it stayed. Some time later, the rest of my collection was shipped to Seoul, where it stayed when I left for America. In 1941 it was seized and paid for by the Japanese government as 'enemy alien property' after they had declared war on America. I understand the collection was given to some college in Korea. I felt glad that other students could benefit from it.

Returning to Devon, near a village called Rousdon on the south coast between Lyme Regis and Beer, is the Slip, where about a century earlier a large part of the cliff slipped down to the beach, revealing a huge variety of ammonites of the Liassic period of the Earth's geological history, ranging in size from truck tyres to pin heads. After scrambling down the rugged cliff path, being ill-equipped and too tired to take the tyre-sized ones, I settled for a stone full of the pin-head size. Years later some well equipped German geologists with pneumatic drills removed the truck-tyre sized ammonites.

Curiously there was a large estate at the top of that cliff above the Slip in Rousdon. Back in about 1900 someone had taken advantage of a shipwreck at the bottom of the cliff bearing a cargo of marble from Italy. They built some fine houses and other buildings with it.

After I left All Hallows, George Shallow found this estate for sale, bought it, and moved the school there where it stayed from 1936 until the school closed for lack of funds 62 years later, after centuries of existence.

Though the school closed 10 years ago as I write this in 2008 the Old Honitonians Club still runs and thanks to the internet I was able to find that Gordon Davidson (the son of Harry Davidson, a great friend of our family in Korea and co-owner of our family gold mine in Eum Chum Khol, North Korea), who had gone to All Hallows shortly after I arrived, had his sons follow him to the school.

During my last term at All Hallows, I had one last duty to perform in the OTC. One evening after we had retired to bed our housemaster came to tell us that he had just heard the news on the wireless that King Edward VIII had abdicated to marry Mrs Wallis Simpson. The next morning the Mayor of Honiton, flanked by an Honour Guard of four tall OTC Cadets, three English and one American, read the Royal Proclamation of Abdication. I was the American!

10

Return To Dilkusha

During the summer holidays Mum and I went to the other end of the Liassic belt that runs across England in a south-west to north-east direction. We spent a fortnight at Robin Hood's Bay, south of Whitby in Yorkshire, where there are masses of ammonites & belemnites in the shale of the beach, solidified mud from ancient seas of the same period found on the shores of Lyme Regis in Dorset. Walking along the cliff-top path northwards to Whitby we encountered – and Mum painted – the ruined abbey founded by St Hilda in 657 AD.

St Hilda's symbol is composed of three ammonites, as she was credited with turning a plague of snakes into stone. The 'snakes' were sea snails, fossil ammonites found in their thousands on the beach below which had lived on a sea bed there millions of years before St Hilda was born. St Hilda's propagandists had no knowledge of geology! Once we went even further north up the Yorkshire coast to Staithes, where I found an excellent shell fossil of a later geological period.

During that holiday Mum and I read *The Saga of the Comstock Lode* which told of the mining history of Virginia City, Nevada, where Dad lived his early life. She told me about Dad and his father and their lives in the gold mines of North Korea, thus preparing me for my return to Korea and my introduction to the family gold mining business, for Dad and his friend Harry Davidson, generally known as Davie, were co-owners of a little mine in the Silver Working Valley of North Korea, called Eum Chum Khol in Korean.

At the end of the holidays, Mum returned to Korea and I started a course in business training at the Reading School of Typing and Shorthand and in 1937 a course on driving. In April 1937 my return to Korea was booked, warm clothes were bought for the icy cold winters and packed in a blue steamer trunk with a red stripe around it for easy identification. On the last night at The Cabin Uncle Ron took me outside, pointed to the moon and said that although we would be far apart we would both be able to see the same moon.

In those days rapid communication was only by cablegram, for which you paid by the word. We really take for granted our computers and the internet these days.

* * * *

My last night in England for many years to come was spent at Mrs Sydney Aris's home, a former summer house of King George III in Lyndhurst, Hampshire. The following day I boarded a Cunard White Star liner, possibly the *Britannic*, or a similar ship, after saying goodbye to my dear Uncle and Aunt who had brought me up in the ways of the English in the land of my ancestors, which I had grown to love as my own. I sailed from Southampton and out into the English Channel with increasing pitching and rolling from the sea as we passed Cornwall and the Isles of Scilly, then on to Cork, in Ireland, to pick up more passengers. Next we braved the tossing waves of the Atlantic. Five days later we entered St Lawrence River, the pathway of early settlers to Canada, stopping first at Quebec and disembarking at Montreal.

Farewell Photo, Uncle Ron, myself & Aunt Mary

Here I was met by friends of my Mother's who guided me to the railway station to get the train to Vancouver. Immigration officers had delayed the ship at Quebec dealing with some other passengers, so we missed the Express and got the slow Trans-Canada train. This turned out to be even more interesting as I saw many fascinating sights such as the hilly eastern provinces and the flat middle prairie lands.

Carrying my Underwood portable typewriter with me, I described the scenes we passed through. One night in the prairies the train had stopped in the middle of nowhere, and the guard returning to the train remarked: "The lights are bright tonight."

Seeing that we were nowhere near a town I wondered what he was talking about. Then, looking out, I saw the Northern Lights like great curtains of light moving across the sky!

At another point in our prairie progress we had a two and a half hour layover in Winnipeg, which to me, after England, looked just like an American city, but I was relieved to see the King and Queen's portraits in the Post Office window: I was still in British territory as far as I was concerned, such was the influence of my British education. On a tip from the guard, when we stopped at Medicine Hat, Alberta, I walked down the track, photographed a local lake and returned before the train resumed its westward progress. I could not have done that on the Express!

I recall a point when the train was slowly climbing through the Rockies, looking straight down as we emerged from a tunnel we could see the tail end of the same train entering the same circular tunnel! The land rose to high, rugged mountains as we progressed through Alberta and then even more so in British Columbia. My spirits rose to greet them! Why? Why had I always yearned for mountains in the dozen years away from the land of my birth?

After about a week on the train, I was met in Vancouver by the American Consul and his wife, friends of Mum's, and stayed with them. While there I posted letters typed on the train, describing the scenes I had observed to friends and relations back in England. Several days later the *Empress of Russia*, a Canadian Pacific liner, left on a two-week voyage to Japan, via the North Pacific Great Circle route, passing the Aleutian Islands on the way. Over five years later Japanese troops invaded those same American islands that we were seeing from the ship's rail. The Japanese were in time expelled by American forces. Sixty-nine years later I flew much of that same route in just 12 hours! Such has been the advance in transportation during my lifetime! Days later, for us on the steamer, a massive mountain rose out of the faint shoreline of Japan. Mount Fuji, Japan's sacred mountain stood as a sentinel behind Yokohama, guiding us into port.

Mr and Mrs Fred Ells, friends of Una's from Standard Oil, picked me up and I stayed with them for a day or two. During that time they took me to the Dai Butsu (the Great Buddha of Kamakura). This was where Dad had proposed to Mum. I continued my epic journey by train to Shimonoseki to take the ferry to Busan (Fusan) at the south-eastern tip of Korea. The next morning, as the overnight ferry came to the land, I saw after 12 years the mountainous land I had always longed for.

Korea! Range after range of mountains. The Land of the Morning Calm was its ancient name. But to me it was the land of my birth, my home, that I had longed for all my young life.

And looking down at the quay as we came alongside was my father, who had made all this adventuring possible, whom I had not seen in eight years! Reunited, we boarded the train for Seoul, known in the days of Japanese rule as Keijo, the Fortified Capital, because it was encircled by its own city wall.

We travelled northwards for several hours with a wide green plain, the rice bowl of Korea, beside us. There were yet more mountains beyond the plain to the west, mountains to the east of us, mountains here and mountains there. On arrival in Seoul's European-styled station, with its central domed roof, I noticed as the train was slowing down that there were boards bearing the name Keijo in English and what looked like Chinese. My father confirmed that it was indeed Chinese which the Japanese also used, calling it Kanji. Educated Koreans understood it but pronounced it quite differently. The train halted just outside the Great South Gate, with its up-turned roofs, and massive stone work, pronounced Nandaimon in Japanese. The Korean version was slightly different – Nandaemun.

We were met by Mum, Mr Kim, Mr Lee, Mr Wong and the rest of the staff of W W Taylor & Co. The taxi driver was told: "Drive to *Kyoson-cho, ichi-banchi.*" Number one, Kyoson Road.

He looked puzzled, so the request was rephrased: "*Tayra San no uchi.*" Mr Taylor's house.

He brightened up and replied in Japanese: "*Hai, wakarimasu.*" ("Yes, I understand.") The large red-brick house on the mountainside above the city could easily be seen from much of the city.

We crossed the city and drove up the mountain road to Dilkusha's gate. Hearing the taxi's horn, Mr Kim, the gate keeper, and Kongsaban, the coolie, hastened to swing wide the gates to Dilkusha's garden. The taxi swept up the tree-lined curving driveway, passed beneath the branches of the fabled ginkgo tree to halt in front of the granite steps of the house that had risen like a phoenix from its ashes. Dilkusha, the Palace of Heart's Delight. A wolf pack assaulted the taxi, barking wildly, tails wagging. Well, they were not wolves, but the family's Alsatians, Jaegar and Rin Tin.

11

The Land Of The Morning Calm As A Japanese Province (1937-1940)

A dozen years had fled. The wanderer was home, home from the Halls of Learning. I had left as a child and returned, shortly after my 18th birthday, as a young man. Here, apparently, I was to spend my life, following my father and grandfather, mining the minerals of this ancient land. Years of my life had been spent away from home and parents with but glimpses of my mother and a longer time still from the land of my birth. So I knew little of my parents' background and what brought them to live in Korea. So shortly after I returned to Dilkusha I asked my father what brought him to Korea.

He replied: "My Grandfather, who evidently descended from the Cameron clan, left Scotland for Nova Scotia, which is Latin for New Scotland. He settled in Antigonish, which is where my father George Alexander Taylor was born. He became a millwright of stamp mills used for grinding ore to a fine powder to enable gold extraction.

"Following the gold rushes of the times in western America,

where millwrights must have been in demand, he moved there, first to Nevada, then Alaska and finally Korea. He was a very good and thorough millwright, too. He probably met my mother, Marietta Lord, who was from Vermont, in Nevada. I was born in Silver City, in that state.

"Later we moved to Virginia City. Then to Alameda, California, where Dad bought us a nice house on Park Avenue, a tree-lined street with good-sized houses surrounded by gardens. When he went to Alaska he built a 500 stamp mill, then the world's largest. My mother became a school teacher and the three children, myself, Bill and Olive, grew up in our home.

"Next Dad went to Korea in 1896. I graduated as a mining engineer from the University of California and joined him a year later. My brother Bill followed later still. We worked with Dad until his death in 1908 then we moved south to start the Chiksan Gold Mining Company.

"It was when I went to Japan to order a gold dredge to be sent from California that I met your mother, and proposed to her saying that I would follow her to India, where she was going next, and marry her as soon as my dredge was running."

Turning to my mother I asked her where her home had been and what brought her to Japan when Dad went there?

She replied: "I was born in Malmesbury, Wiltshire, in England – one of five children, two brothers and two sisters, our father, Doctor Charles Forbes Mouat-Biggs, whose family was traced back to King Henry II of England, and our mother, Mary Louisa Tickell, whose family was traced back to a family who for four generations had been

Lords Lieutenant of Ireland, the English King's personal representative in Ireland.

"Some years after my birth we moved to Cheltenham, in Gloucestershire, where I attended the Ladies' College. Our father and my brothers, Ron and Eric, went into the British Army at the start of World War I to France. Eric was killed during the war. Our mother became a nurse and Una a motorcycle dispatch rider. My elder sister, Betty, and I become actresses and eventually joined a travelling stock company going to India and the Far East, including Japan, where I met Dad and later married him in India."

* * * *

With my increasing maturity I observed the region beyond our home, and how the Japanese rulers forced the Koreans into a Japanese mould in their own land. Place names were in Japanese. At that time, the three contiguous countries of China, Korea and Japan all used Chinese characters for writing but often pronounced them quite differently while retaining the same meaning. Seoul, the Korean name for the capital, meant just that. The Japanese, referring to the wall encircling the city, called it Keijo, the Fortified Capital. They called the country Chosen.

Each small section of the city had a local policeman who knew his area and could keep track of the activities of the Koreans. Houses being numbered in the order they were built, in the Japanese fashion, often meant there was no order to their location so one had to consult the local policeman and his map, enabling him to keep track of local activities.

When Mum put on a Korean play in our garden the policeman was soon there to stop the un-Japanese activity!

Another aspect of this control was apparent in the railway stations, Japanese had to be spoken to acquire tickets and the policemen on the platforms would ask where travellers were going and when they would return.

Beneath Mount Imwangsan, beside the city wall, stood Dilkusha, our rebuilt home, and the famed ancient, giant ginkgo tree. Among ourselves, we had named this mountain Pulpit Rock. In the mornings on our hillside we heard the gongs of the Buddhist temple above us, and on Sundays the bells of the Christian churches below us, sounds of the ancient and modern religious introductions to Korea. Mountains to the north of us, mountains to the south-east and south-west of us.

In the valleys below, the city was sunk in a smoky sea as the early morning rice-cooking fires were lit for the white-clothed Koreans' morning meal. The same fires heated rooms next to the kitchens of the thrifty Koreans. To the south-east, the river Han glinted in the early morning sunshine. To the south-west, white steps climbed up Namsan, South Mountain, to the imported Japanese National Shinto religion and its shrine. As Japan advanced towards war, first with China and then World War II, this religion was forced on the natives of Korea.

Telephone operators spoke Japanese, so one had to use it. After 67 years I still recall our office number: "*Issen sambyku, hachi-ju sam ban.*" 1383. There were no phones where our house was so we had to rely on *pingees* – notes delivered by Kongsaban, our coolie.

Flags were flown everywhere on the many holidays, even on trams: Japanese flags, of course – Korean flags were banned! And the people continued to work. A Korean friend of ours had a Korean flag hidden above the ceiling of his living room, so he lived all his life under his own country's flag. On entering a gymnasium you first bowed to the Emperor's picture. Schools taught Japanese only. Koreans were to take Japanese names and use their religion, although they could practise other religions at the same time. The fine stores, hotels and European-style government buildings were all Japanese. Signs were in Japanese.

In the native quarter open-fronted Korean shops used Hangul, the native phonetic alphabet. I studied Japanese as our family businesses, import-export and mining, were mainly dealing with Japanese authorities and laws. It became my second language and was unexpectedly useful after I left Korea.

12

The Fortified Capital

After rising and dressing each morning, Mum and I would go out and release her dark brown Alsatian, Jaegar, and then his grey son, my dog, Rin Tin, from their dog runs and say "Walk!" and pick up their leads.

At this the dogs would go wild with delight. Leaving the house and passing the giant ginkgo tree as we went up the path to the side gate, just beyond the strawberry beds, with each dog walking to heel beside his respective owner, we went out onto the path beside the decapitated city wall leading toward Pulpit Rock, high above the city.

Rin Tin & I on the altar next to the Ginkgo Tree

Mary Linley Taylor (my mother) holding her dog "Jaegar."

Here and there among young pine tree-covered hillside I noticed some dwarf oaks with amazingly large leaves. The pines had been planted by order of the Japanese authorities. They had established 1 April as Arbor Day when school children went out and planted seedlings on the hillsides. Prior to this programme there had been extensive flood damage each year in the rainy season.

While walking up this wooded hillside we would take time to teach Rin Tin various commands, calling: "Sit," "Lie down," and "Stay." The canine instructions were demonstrated by

Jaegar who knew and acted on these commands instinctively, giving his son an example to follow.

Once we reached Pulpit Rock we would rest awhile and look down at Peking Pass Road and its steep valley. In days and centuries gone by the Annual Tribute Caravan passed through here on its long overland journey to Peking, now known as Beijing, as Korea was then a vassal state protected by China. From here, much of Seoul could be seen, even to the waters of the Han sparkling in the distance.

Then we returned home. On reaching the house we would feed the dogs, then when called they bounded into the house to their assigned corners and stayed there until after breakfast. In each room of the house in which they were allowed they had been trained to go to an assigned corner where they stayed until we called them away.

Sometime after breakfast, I would get out my bicycle and, with Rin Tin running at my side, ride down to the W W Taylor & Co office near the end of Hasegawa-cho, opposite the Chosen Hotel. Rin Tin would lie quietly next to my desk until it was time to return home for lunch.

Later, Jaegar joined our daily trips with a lead strapped to his harness as he was not so good at consistently following beside the bicycle. Unfortunately he was given to suddenly stopping without warning, which would derail me and my bicycle. Solution? Give the lead to Rin Tin who kept his father in tow!

Almost the entire journey to the office was downhill, so for me it was a matter of coasting, using my bells and brakes as needed. Japanese bicycles had bell clappers mounted on springs, and when a lever on the handle bars was pulled back an extension of the clapper mounted on a spring engaged with the wheel spokes, repeatedly ringing the bell placed next to it, making a sound like a noisy alarm clock. I had two of them to double the sound!

On reaching the office both dogs would lie quietly next to my desk until the lunch time return home.

The office was situated in the business district of Seoul, where I gained a concept of how this family business operated. It appeared to have imported almost everything under the sun. If you wanted it, W W Taylor & Co had it – or could get it. I found American cars, English house paint, New Zealand insurance, Ingersoll watches, Underwood typewriters, 20th Century Fox films for rent and Korean curios for sale to name a few items.

Much of the imports the company had distributed were sharply curtailed as Japan continued its invasion of China, and the chief income came from importing and renting 20th Century Fox films, which were in high demand by various movie houses. Japanese propaganda films were not very popular with the Koreans, I expect.

There were also some quite exotic Korean curios for sale, including black lacquer screens, chests and tables with Korean scenes portrayed in inlaid Mother of Pearl derived from precisely cut abalone shell. Also brass butterfly palace candlesticks, brass bowls and much more besides. These were for sale under the direction of Kim Chusa, whose name was an exalted title afforded to him by virtue of being the former keeper of King Kojong's treasures.

The Japanese had offered him an illustrious position in their government, but he declined to work for the usurpers of his land. During World War II they threw him in prison and returned him to his home on a *jiggy* – a framework of stout sticks, worn by a man in the manner of a knapsack – as an insult when he was dying. Unknown to them he was the one who had lived under his country's flag. It was found inside the ceiling of his house after his death.

When the time for the midday meal approached, on looking down on the street, one could see some skilled cyclists, delivering stacked circular *bentos* – lunch boxes – which they balanced on one hand while they guided their bikes with the other, dodging in and out of traffic.

Besides learning the family business, I also started learning the ways of life in the Japanese empire. Little did anyone guess in 1937 that its days were numbered, and eight years later, South Korea, at least, would be free, while North Korea would be enslaved in a Korean copy of Soviet Russia.

Hasegawa-cho, named after a Japanese Governor-General, was a street of European-style office buildings some five or six storeys high. At one end stood the Japanese Railways Chosen Hotel – a convenient stopping place for tourists. Across the street was W W Taylor & Co with a shop full of Korean curiosities, especially attractive to tourists!

At the other end the road led to a wide-open area in front of the General Post Office, next to which was the entrance to the all Japanese street, Honmachi, then the huge Misukoshi department store, forming the far side of this open area. From here, a road named Nandaimon-dori ran down to Nandaimon, the Great South Gate. Honmachi was filled with fascinating shops with exotic clothes, lacquerware, chinaware and all manner of works by Japanese craftsmen, as well as modern radio, hardware and camera shops, restaurants and geisha houses. On this street the only permitted wheeled traffic were rickshaws for the sole use of geishas.

Opposite the South Gate was the large red-brick Severance Presbytarian Medical College Hospital, where I was born in 1919 just before Emperor Kojong's funeral – when my family members took actions which had a marked effect on Korea's history.

When my father first came to Korea the city walls completely encircled Seoul, and the gates were shut at night. Returning late one night from a party, Dad had to find a place to climb over the wall.

Nandaimon was enclosed by a low wall so traffic went around instead of through its central opening. Across the street was the domed roof of Seoul railway station. All our travels in to and out of Korea started or ended here. Road transport was little used, for outside the city the roads were for the most part unpaved.

Unlike train travel in Western lands, where once you bought your ticket you waited undisturbed on the platform for your train, in Korea under Japanese rule you would be questioned by the platform policeman as to where you were going, what you were going to do and when you would return.

They practised their fragmentary English on me. Once, I was asked if I drank tobacco! I found that the equivalent Japanese phrase uses a word for 'drink' rather than a word for 'smoke'. As my knowledge of Japanese improved I would turn the tables and practise my Japanese on them, telling them of our travel plans.

* * * *

Another aspect of local culture that I found useful was a course in judo at the local *kodokwan*, or judo gym, where almost all the other students were Japanese policemen. One day a local Japanese language newspaper had a headline about an American who was learning "the spirit of Bushido, the way of the warrior". That was news to me, for I was the American, and was merely learning judo as a method of self-defence.

In the various lands in which I have studied I have found varying ways of showing respect to the ruling powers. American children pledge allegiance to the flag; British children sing God Save the Queen. On entering the *kodokwan*, students got down on all fours and bowed, head to the floor in front of a picture of His Majesty, the Japanese Emperor. Some missionaries objected to this form of salute, but I personally felt that as this was the Japanese custom I would follow it out of politeness.

After the salute we would go to our assigned places in the hall and change into judo clothes. If we desired to have a bout with another student we would walk over to face them and get down just as we did for the emperor's picture and bow in like manner. After the match we would both bow again. Customs vary so much in different countries and what is normal in one may be considered quite shocking in another.

This brings to mind an event in the *kodokwan* and another that occurred on a beach in Japan. When the session was over, everyone removed all their clothes and went to the nicely lit bathroom with clear glass windows looking out on to the street.

One day when the young policemen, *sans* clothes, were having a water-fight in the bathroom, a beautifully attired Japanese girl came along and enjoyed the spectacle. No one was the least concerned about their nudity.

On another occasion, a number of Japanese were cavorting in the nude on a seaside beach, but when they attempted to enter the water a nearby policeman informed them they had to have bathing suits on to do that!

Having glimpsed some of the down town sights that attracted me, let's return to 110 Hasegawa-cho – the Taylor building – and assume this to be an ordinary day at lunch, when I would be returning home with my canine companions, Rin Tin and Jaegar. We would head north with the City Hall to our left and further on would pass near Toksu Palace, which was then a public park with a beautiful garden, not far from the Anglican Catheral of St Nicholas. Then bearing north-east we would enter the rather dark, high-walled Legation Street. Some way up this street the walls disappeared and the low Korean-style building of the United States Consulate General was revealed.

Further up the road was the Seoul Foreign School, then the former Czarist Russian Embassy and its Russian Orthodox Church with its onion-shaped dome and curious double cross. Next, Seidaimon-dori, the wide road leading to the region of the Great West Gate, Seidaimon. Crossing this road, we reached the hill up to Dilkusha. From this point the road narrowed and twisted its way upwards, so I dismounted and pushed the bicycle.

Further up hill was a stone-mason's yard where patient Korean masons slowly ground down blocks of granite, presumably for tombstones. They would even engrave

English lettering on them if one desired. I presume they used stencils to get the letters correctly cut. This brings to mind a case of an English language tombstone being cut in a Korean stonemason's yard where the similarity of 'b' and 'd' went unnoticed. The completed tombstone asserted that the occupant was born twice, but never died!

English was ostensibly taught in the schools, but few Koreans that I have met have had much luck with our confusing language. As far as I know the old teaching methods are still used today, with rather poor results. Quite a few Koreans who can afford it send their children to learn our language in countries where it is spoken as in Canada and America.

Here and there throughout Asia, one came across curiously constructed English signs which either made no sense at all or were downright funny without meaning to be. Further up the same road that my dogs and I were ascending there was one of the first category. Outside a shop that apparently sold natural mineral water was a picture of a Korean girl holding aloft a bottle, with a sign proclaiming: *"The wonderful good for Mineral Spring."*

Further along, the road went downhill a way, revealing some American missionary houses to the left in the dell and Dilkusha and its ginkgo tree towering above them on the mountainside. We climbed the hill, passed through the gate and were soon home.

On Sundays, Mum and I walked downhill with the dogs at our sides, on the same route – down Legation Street past the US Consulate General, then left uphill and a short cut through the British Consulate General grounds to the Anglican Cathedral of St Nicholas next door to attend Holy Communion in the crypt. The dogs were told to stay in a shady corner and we entered the small chapel where Bishop Cecil Cooper conducted the service in English, with additions in Japanese or Korean for communicants of those races. In contrast, in the main cathedral upstairs the service was conducted entirely in Korean.

Our dogs had been well trained to remain lying down when given the command "stay". However, once after Mum had been away a long time at our family gold mine in North Korea, the dogs and I met her going into church. And at about the time of the sharing of the bread and wine, Jaegar had waited long enough and quietly walked up the aisle and lay beside Mum as the Bishop was giving her communion.

* * * *

In keeping with the Japanese control of Korea, I started taking a class in their language, conducted by a Japanese teacher. But later through our friends Gerald and Aline Phipps, the British Consul-General and his wife, we found an excellent tutor in Chris Hupfer, a German professor in a Japanese University. Chris understood the problems foreign students had with Japanese, and was able to make its study far more meaningful.

Besides Chinese characters, written vertically, Japanese had two alphabets – Hiragana and Katakana – the latter used chiefly for approximating foreign words like bus (*ba-su*) and beer (*bi-ru*). When it was written horizontally on containers one had to read it both ways to see which way made sense! At that time there appeared to be no rule as to the reading direction, which could cause confusion. A case in point was when metal containers were unavailable a brand of metal polish called Ruby was put out in beer bottles. So was it *ru-bi* or *bi-ru*?!

Chris became a good family friend, interested in hiking, rock climbing, skiing, sailing and swimming. So we arranged hiking, rock climbing and sailing excursions in the summer with him, along with skiing in the winter. My Aunt Una became quite enamoured of him, but due to the fact that by 1939 their respective countries were at war, marriage was not feasible.

Censorship of outgoing letters and incoming radio news was another aspect of Japanese control. Short wave sets were illegal, cheap low-power broadcast band sets were legal, and powerful local transmitters blocked signals from abroad. Owners of imported all-band sets had to notify the police to send a radio repairman to cut out the short wave part.

One owner found that his officially fixed set could be unfixed simply by the removal of one screw. So he removed the screw, listened to the BBC news and replaced it afterwards. I found another dodge around the ban – a wave trap article in *Wireless World Magazine* which enabled me to tune out much of the Japanese signals and get broadcasts from Shanghai, which re-broadcast short wave newscasts from KGEI in San Francisco. When the news came on, Mum and I would arm ourselves with pen and paper and write down everything we could hear, comparing notes afterwards to get a fair idea of the uncensored news of the world.

* * * *

Sunday walks with the Phipps would begin with us being transported across town in the chauffeur-driven consular car to the foot of our desired mountain and we would be met at the end of the walk with the same car to return us to our homes. On some occasions we went for a cruise on the river Han in a boat owned by a young Frenchman named

Claude, whose boat was driven by a petrol (gasoline) engine mounted with an adaptor which allowed the use of wood from which gas was derived to run the engine. This device was increasingly used on trucks and buses because of the shortage of petrol for civilian use.

On one occasion I went with a YMCA missionary, Gordon Avison, in his car for about 300 miles from Seoul down to Kwanju province. Quite a ride! The car's springs had been repaired by welding. And the unpaved roads beyond Seoul soon unwelded them! Gordon also had a couple of Korean hunters with him who would get him to stop for them to open fire on game birds whenever they saw them. At the end of the trip, quite late at night, we came to his house with an assortment of 13 different game birds.

At another time my mother, Chris and I went down from Chemulpo, now called Inchon, and took a ship to the port for Kwangwha Island where we walked inland to a Buddhist monastery. We spent the night there, ate seaweed and rice for breakfast then returned to the ferry for the journey home. Inchon has the most tremendous tides, much like those on the Bay of Fundy, between Nova Scotia and New Brunswick in Canada. The ferry could only make the trip at high tide, as there was nothing but mud between Kwangwha and Inchon at low tide.

This was effective many years later in the Korean War. The Communists, who had driven the Allies down to Busan, had a defence line on the edge of Seoul. Knowing about these tremendous tides they assumed nobody would land there, so didn't fortify it. General MacArthur also knew about these tides and performed one of his characteristic attacks behind enemy lines, landed at Inchon and trapped a North Korean Army as a result of landing behind them.

Returning to the Seoul of 1937, the Seoul Union, a club started by missionaries, had a bowling alley and tennis courts. The courts were flooded in winter, thus forming skating rinks. Skilled skaters, however, went to the frozen river Han. Una, an enthusiastic fan of any sport in spite of an artificial leg acquired following a motorcycle accident while a dispatch rider in World War I in England, insisted on skating too, until she fell and broke her remaining ankle.

When I returned to Korea she was working at the Standard Oil Company office as the manager's secretary. She had first come to Korea to work at W W Taylor & Co. Later in the winter when the rest of us went skiing at Sambo Kyo, a ski resort in what is now North Korea, she went too, using a toboggan that I made for her using canvas and a cut down pair of skis.

The following summer she went sailing in her canoe with Chris Hupfer on the lake at Wha Shin Po, on the east coast of Korea, further south than our original seaside site. Always game for any adventure, Una later organised a trip for herself, Mum and I to Peking (Beijing) just before I returned to America to attend college.

13

Gold Mines In North Korea

The next thing to do was to get some idea of the mining business at the large, advanced American-owned mine and the small, cruder Korean copy in the family-owned mine. So Dad contacted a friend of his at the Oriental Consolidated Mining Company where he was once a mine supervisor for seven years.

Generally known as the OCM, the company was situated in the far north-west of North Korea. It was arranged for me to go up and stay with his friend and his wife for a time to see a modern mine and its workings. I took the train to a station a little north of Pyengyang, which was said to be about 70 miles south of Unsan, and was driven the rest of the way by car. The mine compound was in a bowl-like valley where the houses of the 50 or so American mine staff lived with a central club house building. There were several different mine tunnels in that area.

I was first taken down a mile-deep shaft in the main mine, where battery-powered locomotives pulled the ore cars and rechargable electric headlamps were worn by the miners who used, I believe, American Ingersoll-Rand compressed air drills to drill the rock for dynamiting.

Going to other mines, I went uphill in a tram at an angle of about 45 degrees. The vehicle was powered by the weight of loaded ore cars going down hill, connected by cables wrapped around a drum at the base of a tower at the top of the hill which then extended to connections on empty cars, some with passengers, which were pulled uphill. A man in a glass-enclosed tower operated brakes to slow the cars.

Ore was taken first to a rock-crushing machine with opposing jaws, driven by a cam to move the jaws in and out. The small resulting pieces were fed into a ball mill which reduced the little pieces to powder, at which point water flowing through the ball mill carried the powder to copper plates amalgamated with mercury.

Gold in the powder was attracted to and stuck on to the mercury, the remaining powder, still with some gold content, went on to the cyanide plant which dissolved the gold and then passed through tanks containing zinc which replaced the gold from the cyanide solution and precipitated it as a black powder. This, when melted down, was reduced to gold bars weighing 52 pounds.

These were then delivered to the local post office, which was remarkably elaborate for such an out of the way place. Its almost sole job was to transport gold from this mine. All gold had to be sold to the Japanese government, whose job it was to protect its shipping. Prior to Japanese control of Korea, gold had to be shipped out under armed guard, and once some bandits had attacked a shipment, but after seriously wounding a guard who later died, they were driven off.

A simpler way before the establishment of the post office was for one strong man to carry two bars in a suitcase and

take the train. At 104 pounds, few people could get very far
with it!

* * * *

On return to Seoul, having seen the latest mining methods
available in Korea, I needed to see the lower-scale methods
used at the family-owned mine in Eum Chum Khol, the
Silver Working Valley in North Korea.

It was my birthday some time after returning to Dilkusha
and I was given a clinometer in an nice leather case and
strap, a most useful instrument in the mining business. It is
used for measuring angles of rock strata and mineral veins
to determine where one might be able to tap into them at
a lower or higher point if needed. Another family member
had a different idea for the uses of the clinometer's leather
case and strap. He chewed it! So I had Rin Tin's signature
on my new clinometer case – luckily not on the instrument
inside!

Not long after my return to Seoul, an opportunity came up
the see the family-owned mine. One day, when my father
was going to be away for some time on a business trip, he
suggested that my Mother and I visit the family mine at
Eum Chum Khol. Its Japanese name was Heiko Kogyo
Kabushiki Kaisha, translated into English as Heiko County
Gold Mining Co Ltd.

He also suggested that while there I should see if I could
trace the white quartz boulders that were in the south end
of the north-south valley above the large bridge that led to
the mine compound. As quartz is the only rock in which
gold is known to occur, finding its source could well lead to
another gold strike!

Dad arranged for Woghn San, our smart Korean accountant who spoke Korean, Japanese and English at W W Taylor & Co, to send a telegram to Won Tal Ho, the Korean mine manager, that he should be ready to conduct us around all the facilities of the mine. In this age of telephones and computers that would be simple. But in Korea – especially North Korea – in the 1930s it was a little more complex.

A letter could be sent, but would take perhaps a week or more to reach its destination, so we used the rapid means of communication. All my father had to do was write a note in English, call Nam Doo, the cook, to tell Konsabun, the coolie, to take a *pingee* (a note) to Woghn San at the office. The coolie walked a couple of miles or so down town to the Taylor building on Hasegawa-cho (River Valley Road) and delivered the note. Woghn San then went to the post office and sent a telegram to Hong Kil Tong, our Korean agent in Sambo Kyo (Medicine Spring) the nearest railway station to the mine. Then Hong would employ either a coolie or a *mafu* (horseman) and pony going that way to carry another *pingee* over the mountains and valleys to Won Tal Ho at the mine office. That's all!

So, the three of us headed for Seoul railway station. *Three of us?* Yes, of course, we had our faithful companion Rin Tin with us. Jaegar stayed at Dilkusha to look after the house and grounds and the servants looked after his needs. We had found from past experience to leave one member of our canine police force on guard when we went away, for the only time we had a break in was when there was no resident dog. In those days there was a saying among the foreigners in Korea that many of the poor people of the land, having next to nothing of their own, would steal anything not nailed down – and the nails if it was nailed down! The presence of a large, wolf-like dog discouraged such ideas.

After Rin Tin was established in his special compartment (dog-box) we boarded the train headed for Wonsan (Gensan), stopping at Sambo Kyo. After travelling several hours from Seoul we passed the extensive rice paddies of the central rice bowl area of Korea, then headed into the northern mountains and seemingly countless tunnels. Hurtling out of one such tunnel we came to a halt in a steep-sided valley with tall dark mountains all round. We had finished the first part of our journey.

This was Sambo Kyo, in North Korea. Here Rin Tin joined us on the platform and was surrounded by a circle of Koreans wondering what this wolf was doing there. Then they were amazed to see him obey silent signals with my hand or quietly spoken commands to walk to heel beside me as we left the station.

Knowing that the next and last segment of the journey took five hours it was deemed best not to attempt to cover this considerable distance the same day. Instead we spent the night in the nearby Eastern Sea Hotel, the best in town. It was but a few steps from the station, so we stretched our legs and walked there.

Our baggage came later by the usual form of transport – a man carrying it on a *jiggy*. From the back it was shaped like a double-barred A, not quite closed at the top. A couple of stout wooden branches projected backwards from the A-frame at 45 degrees. Upon this a flexible wicker basket could be laid for carrying earth or stones, for example. When it was being loaded it could be supported like a tripod with the addition of a long, thick stick with a Y-shaped top end which engaged one of the cross bars. Without the wicker basket it could carry such items as planks or baggage, as it did now.

We found the Eastern Sea Hotel to be equipped with all the modern conveniences of up-to-date hotels of the 1930s in North Korea. This hotel was so advanced for its time and place because Sambo Kyo not only had a mineral hot spring, for which it was named, but was also popular as a ski resort in the winter.

There was central heating, hot and cold running water and air conditioning. The rooms were wired for light as well. Hot baths of Japanese design and manufacture, rare in much of Korea at the time, were also available. The beds were comfortable, with easily adjustable heat, and came with a variety of pillows. There was no problem with the menus either, as the management went out of their way to be sure guests knew what was on the day's menu even though they might not be good Korean linguists.

Some of the hotel's amenities may need a little explanation for those not used to the delights of up-country travel in North Korea. Let's look at that list again.

Central heating was common to most Korean houses, where the smoke of the kitchen fire passed under the floor of the room next to it, the floor being made of low stone walls capped with stone slabs to form tunnels under the floor which was covered with mud which in turn was covered with thick paper nicely polished with cow dung.

As for hot and cold running water, well, the cold water did run, in the creek below the hotel! The hot – or rather warm – water came in a kettle in the morning from the kitchen to the tin basins set out in the courtyard horse-trough for those guests who thought washing was necessary before breakfast.

Hot baths, which were a rarity in much of Korea at the time, were also said to be available. However as few had such baths, few saw the need to use them and when my mother checked out this new facility one winter, she found the contents of this so called hot tub was a solid block of ice.

Wired for light means there was a bare galvanized iron wire from one corner of the room to the other on which a paraffin (kerosene) lamp was hung. This was a vast improvement on the saucer of bean oil on the floor with a wick floating in it, which was the style prior to installation of modern wiring.

Air conditioning: if the room became too hot and stuffy, you simply poked your finger through the closed window to let a little cold night air in. It was painless as the pane was made of paper!

As we slept on the floor, all we had to do to adjust the heat was to slide around until we found a comfortable spot, using the supplied Japanese futon above or below as needed! The variety of pillows suited a variety of tastes: a bag of rice husks for softies, or the more common adjustable pillow for the tougher types. This one was a low, rectangular piece of wood and different heights were obtainable by turning it around. Being Western softies we brought our own! (Pillows, that is!)

No problem with the menus. Even if you couldn't read Korean. Menus? There were none, and my mother once stayed at this hotel for six weeks and never was at a loss as to what was on the menu. It was the same for all meals! For all six weeks! After 69 years I can't say I remember the entire menu, but there was a large wooden box with a lid for the rice and numerous smaller bowls of things like inch-long fish, seaweed, beans boiled in sugar water, octopus, sea slugs and the like.

In the morning, following ablutions in the horse-trough outside, we retired to our rooms and consumed breakfast, which was delivered to our doors, identical to supper the night before. When finished we got ready to leave and listened for the tinkle, or rather the clonk, of pony bells made of crudely shaped sheet metal. This was supposed to frighten away tigers which were credited with being on the loose in the surrounding hills. These bells were borne by our rapid transit little Manchurian ponies, led by Korean *mafu*s (horsemen).

Our baggage was loaded on to the ponies along with a Western saddle which we kept at Sambo Kyo in case anyone wanted to ride. This was put onto one pony. So we headed out down the street then up the long zigzag path by which we slowly ascended the first bleak mountain barrier, with Rin Tin walking at my side and the *mafu*s and ponies strung out behind.

Reaching the summit at last, Mum pointed first to the path that led down into the next valley, with a stream sparkling in the sunshine at its foot.

"Look at the wonderful new road we had built," she said proudly.

"What road?" I asked.

All I could see was a path with rocks and bushes diverting its course here and there. It was wide enough for the ponies and perhaps a bicycle if carefully steered around the rocks that stuck out of the so-called road. I had just come from the well-paved roads of England, and didn't appreciate that a track too narrow for even a small car could be a road at all.

My father on a wide patch of this "road" while on an earlier visit to our mine in Eum Chum Khol, North Korea.

Raising my eyes I could see row after succeeding row of bleak, treeless mountains. Mum pointed to the most distant range and told me that we had to get to it before nightfall.

"My goodness, it will take a week at least to get there," I thought to myself.

These bare mountain sides were quite like those that some of the earliest American missionaries saw on the hills around Inchon (Jinsen) and Seoul when they arrived in the 1890s – in contrast to the tree-covered slopes around Seoul which had been planted during the Japanese occupation.

We made our way down the wandering path to walk beside the stream and every so often the path crossed the water course by a variety of modern bridges. Well, they were modern in the sense that they had been constructed earlier the same year, but not quite what people of Western lands would call modern. The first was made of timber, quite the best available for miles around, almost three inches in

103

diameter! Two such timbers lashed together and laid across the boulders in the stream bed were the sole parts of this so-called bridge. My mother managed to get across without falling in. Rin Tin just splashed his way across. And I crossed by hopping from stone to stone. I presume the ponies and the *mafu*s, who were far behind us, just waded across.

The path went on in its erratic course, dodging large boulders and the few bushes which grew in the largely bleak landscape, with some tough grass that was unfit for the ponies to eat, so there was no stalling on the way for them to have a quick snack.

I was intrigued with the golden flecks in the sand of the stream. These were in fact flecks of golden mica washed from the eroded micaschist, a metamorphic rock which abounded in that valley.

Eventually we came to yet another crossing point with another 'modern' bridge which was nice and wide, enabling a swift crossing without fear of falling into the water. It was constructed of locally available materials: bundles of brushwood laid over the narrow stream beds with rocks to hold the sticks down.

The reason the bridges had been constructed so recently was because they were either washed away each year in the rainy season or just removed and used for fuel before the rains had a chance to take them. After about two and a half hours of walking we came to a half-way house, an inn with food for man and beast.

It was built in the traditional Korean fashion, of largely local building materials. It had a straw roof, wood-framed mud walls, and a narrow wooden porch a few feet wide running along its front, about a foot off the ground. This porch, called a *malu*, is where you sat down to remove your shoes before entering the house. You would then open the wood-framed, white, paper-covered doors, which also acted as windows, and, ducking your head to avoid the low overhang of the projecting roof, enter the room.

Its sub-floor heating was of the same type as the Eastern Sea Hotel and just about all other Korean houses of that era. When food was being cooked in hot weather the rest of the family moved out to the *malu*.

The average Korean house had two living rooms and a kitchen in between. Bathrooms were unknown, and not considered necessary at that time and place. In that regard I recall my Aunt Una Mouat-Biggs telling me of a Korean in the 1930s who told her with pride that he hadn't had a bath since the Russo-Japanese War (of 1904-5!)

A common sight outside Korean kitchens were large pickle jars three or four feet high containing *kimchi*, an exceedingly hot peppery pickle and an essential part of the Korean diet.

When the *mafu*s arrived at the half-way house they became embroiled in an argument with the inn-keeper over the price of beans – the necessary ingredients for the ponies' fuel as the grass of the country was unfit for the ponies to eat. When the price and amount had finally been settled the beans had to be cooked to make bean soup, which was cooled and fed to the ponies in lieu of grass. We sat on the *malu* while this was going on and ate the sandwiches we had brought with us, sharing some with Rin Tin.

Then we started up the trail to the mine, leaving the ponies and *mafu*s to catch up when they were ready. At one point the rocky path climbed high above the dashing stream below and Mum pointed out that this was called Mal Gorie (Horse Drop Fall), for a man riding from his wedding fell with his horse and they were both killed on the rocks below.

As we walked along, the sun steadily sank behind the jagged mountains of the steep and increasingly narrow valley, hence the light was decreasing and I was wondering how on earth we were ever going to reach that distant mountain peak, let alone the valley behind. Not far from here we could hear a steady pounding that grew progressively louder as the daylight dimmed, and as we descended to the river, crossed yet another of those modern bridges, we found ourselves in a miners' village with wooden flumes bringing river water to the pounding stamp mills.

Over the rushing torrent of water someone called out: *"Yobosio, yobosio, sayan saram isio, puen isio."* ("Hey there, hey there! The foreigners have come, and the lady has come.")

Lamps bobbed along on the opposite shore and lights blazed forth from several rooms of the buildings. We had arrived, although to me it looked for all the world that there were many more mountains yet to cross.

"No," Mum explained, we were in Eum Chum Khol, the Silver Working Valley. This was far earlier than I could have hoped for. It was the same trick my father had played on my mother when she first came to the mine, now she had passed it on to me! We crossed the only bridge that would support a truck – if the 'road' was ever made wide enough for it to reach this bridge.

As she reached the far side, Mum turned and said: "Welcome to the Silver Working Valley and the land and buildings of our Japanese-named gold mine, the Heiko Kogyo Kabushki Kaisha."

We had arrived at the mine. It had taken us five hours to travel 12 miles! Such was rapid transit in the country districts of North Korea at that time.

In fact, it was no better than in the 1890s when foreigners first came to Korea. The time could be almost halved if you walked without the assistance of ponies and *mafu*s, but then you would have to travel with next to no baggage.

We entered the living quarters, finding them nice and warm. Rin Tin, smart dog that he was, went to a corner next to the stove and lay down as we prepared to take advantage of a great luxury, not to be found for miles around: a hot bath! The sub-floor heater, variously called the kang floor or *ondal* in the bedroom, the wood stove in the office or owner's living quarters and the bath had all been fired up several hours before our arrival, so all were ready for our occupation.

In the bathroom, which led off from the owner's living room-cum-office, through a sliding door, there was a circular cast iron bath tub, its rim level with the cement floor. It had a circular wooden lid. Above it was the source of cold water, a rubber garden hose with a wooden plug in the end. Below the filled tub was its source of heat – a fire underneath, fired from a shed outside. There was a wooden grating at the bottom of the tub to keep one's toes from the hot bottom. To turn on the cold tap you grasped the hose in one hand and bent it, then pulled the plug out with the other, controlling the forceful flow by how much you bent the hose. To stop it, the hose was bent all the way over and the plug jammed back into the end. The other end of the hose was secured, pointing upstream in the wooden flume outside, which brought river water above and behind the bathroom and to the 20 stamp mills, thundering just beyond and below the building.

At Eum Chum Khol a Korean miner panning ground gold ore from mills behind him.

The wooden cover of the bath had a little trap door in the centre so water could be added or ladled out when the bath was not in use. When the tub had been filled with cold water, the lid would be lowered and the fire started beneath the tub. It would be kept burning for a couple of hours before use. To use it in the Japanese fashion, one ladled out some warm water, washed with it, then rinsed off with more, raised the lid and when the temperature had been adjusted by addition of more cold water, one slid carefully into the tub and had a good soak. After both of us had indulged in this Japanese-style luxury, generally quite unknown to the Koreans, we prepared for dinner.

We drew on our stocks of tinned food, heated them on the stove in the corner of the room and had supper, after which we retired to the bedroom where a couple of canvas camp cots provided further luxury. We didn't have to sleep on the floor as the previous night when enjoying the luxury of the Eastern Sea Hotel!

We were gradually lulled to sleep by the unending pounding of the mills which hammered the ore of the mine without ceasing day or night. Day after day and week after week. They only stopped when in need of repair or when the winter frosts finally froze the flume water. When the spring warmth thawed the ice the mills started their unending pounding once more.

Awaking the following morning, we saw the sky and growing light, but no other sign of the sun as the steep treeless sides of the narrow valley precluded it from appearing for some hours to come. After rising and dressing I suggested we continued with our daily routine of a walk with Rin Tin before breakfast and follow Dad's suggestion to see how far the line of white quartz boulders go in the southern end of the north-south valley.

So, strapping on my geological hammer, which I always carried whenever there was chance of rock specimens, I left the owner's quarters with Rin Tin at my side. We passed the mine office, the big bridge and the assay office just south of it and along the path leading up the valley with the rushing torrent beside it.

Looking to the right of the path I saw what appeared to be white quartz boulders and ran over to them, and to my amazement found that they were not white, but a beautiful pink, translucent rose quartz – a semi-precious stone! I gathered some samples and showed them to Mum who suggested we take the samples back and return to our quest later. Lacking any local name we decided on the spot to call this Rose Quartz Valley.

So we returned where Mum, never a proficient cook, was able to fry up some eggs on the stove. I asked her where on earth she got the eggs, and she mentioned she had packed a couple of strings of eggs with our food – the neat Korean way of encasing eggs in straw and tying the straw at both ends of each egg enabled their easy and safe transport. So they were sold by the string of 10 eggs or so.

Breakfast finished and washed up, we decided to visit the mine facilities so Mum went to the mine office and talked to Won Tal Ho, the mine manager, who guided us up the rocky path of the east-west valley, where the main ore lode was situated. The bleak mountain side resembled a Swiss cheese, it was so full of holes.

"What on earth are all those holes for?" I asked.

"They are the tributers' tunnels – they pay a portion of what they mine to the company for the right to mine the rest, like sharecroppers," Mum replied.

"The company has its own tunnel at the base of the lode, going straight into the mountain side and using a rail car to haul out the rock and ore from the mine."

We climbed the erratic paths up the mountain to one of these tunnels. When we were outside the entrance I led Rin Tin aside to a flat spot and told him: "Lie down, and stay."

Thanks to his training he would stay put until we returned.

Won Tal Ho led the way bearing a carbide lamp which gave

a brilliant white light. These tunnels were decidedly low, and I had to use my head to avoid losing my head on the rocky roof. This type of mining work is distinctly uncomfortable for a six-footer like myself, so I crept along, keeping my head well down.

Also, the tunnel twisted and turned and rose and fell as it followed the course of the mineral vein. The Korean tributers used young boys to haul the rock and ore out of the mine in panniers on their backs, so they were not so inconvenienced by the tiny tunnels. Coming at last to the tunnel face, or end, we found miners working in the glare of carbide lamps, hammering long steel drills into the rock face with hand hammers.

Usually, several hours pounding would yield a hole big and long enough for a stick of dynamite to be inserted, then everyone would leave, the fuses lit and the area cleared of miners. The miners returned some considerable time after the explosions to allow the fumes to clear, and they scraped up the shattered rock using a tool rather like half a pickaxe that was as wide as a hoe. The rock was borne out of the mine on the boys' backs.

Coming out we made our way to the company tunnel, with Rin Tin trotting at my side. Again we found a place to have him stay obediently outside while we walked into the dead straight tunnel – where a six footer could walk with ease. Here the vein of quartz running through the granite country rock was clearly visible. Here and there were quite large deposits of galena, lead sulphide with some impurities of both silver and gold – impurities that were worth much more than the abundant lead.

There was also some iron pyrite and chalcopyrite glistening, looking like gold. The first is known as fools' gold, with a brassy colour which is really iron sulphide; the second is similar but has copper in it as well and looks even more like gold. It is extremely rare for gold to occur visibly in its native state, in the surrounding quartz, the only rock that bears it.

Walking beside the rail line, where ore cars took the rock and minerals out of this tunnel, we easily reached the entrance and just outside found a blacksmith's shop where men heated then hammered blunted hand drills to sharpness and re-tempered them for use again. We found that the ore going to the mine compound for further processing was carried in panniers slung on either the sides of bullocks in lieu of trucks, or ore cars. Following the bullocks we walked back, down the steep and narrow path to the main mine compound where the ore was sorted.

Now, let's look at the layout of the mine compound. As stated before it was in a treeless, steep, narrow valley, with a few grasses and little else.

The main office and owner's living quarters ran parallel to the mountain behind it in a more or less north-south direction. The doors and windows, for the most part, faced west across the hard-packed earth, towards a second line of buildings of Korean design. Directly behind these buildings, and separated by only a narrow pathway, was the river, which divided us from the Korean miner's village of Eum Chum Khol.

At the north end of the main mine buildings were the owner's living quarters, where we stayed, and beyond this were the 20 stamp mills which lulled us to sleep the first night. The mine office was at the south end, and like the owner's quarters was an entirely wooden building attached to the purely Korean structure between the wooden ends. Just below the village, the north-south river flowing through our recently named Rose Quartz Valley, joined with an east-west river coming down from the eastern valley which led downhill from the main mineral lode.

The bridge capable of bearing a truck was at the south end of the mine compound, and just south of the road leading from the bridge stood the assay office, where chemical tests could be made to judge the gold and other mineral content of the ore from the mine.

There was a path leading southwards up this valley to a village some miles off. Though we tended to judge distances in miles, the official measurements in Korea were then based on the metric system so the official distance would be in kilometres. However, the local Koreans would consider distances in *li*, which are about a third of a mile.

At the north end of the mine compound were other devices and implements for further processing of the ore. Some for reducing it to a size small enough to put into the mills, and others for subsequent processing. The ore from the mine was first sorted: the grey-black galena (lead sulphide) was put into straw sacks and set aside to be hauled by pony to the railway and thence to the Japanese-run smelter at Chinnampo, in the far north of Korea.

One of two methods could be used to reduce the quartz to pea-sized pieces to prepare it for fine grinding in the stamp mills. At one point there was a sturdy stone column, made up of large chunks of granite cemented together, above which was a large iron weight in the shape of an inverted artillery round *sans* shell, suspended by its point with a strong cable going to a long, large pole set firmly in the ground at about

45 degrees. This allowed the flexible pole to bend and a piece of ore on top of the column could easily be broken by pulling down the weight. Flexing the pole would lift it up again. This had been copied from a device used in California during its gold rush, the idea for which had been brought from Mexico. However, the Koreans, being traditionalists, preferred to sit on the ground and use small hand hammers in their fists to break the ore.

The water-powered mills were copies of the ones that my grandfather had brought to the country in 1896. Essentially these were wooden copies of the mills first used at the OCM. Their overshot water-wheels were driven by flume-borne water tapped into the river higher up the mountain. The water-wheels rotated shafts with wooden projections which engaged with wooden cubes on the sides of the vertical mill shafts, which were lifted and dropped. Their bottom ends fitted into hollow cylinders, the lower parts being solid iron, forming hammers which pounded on solid iron anvils beneath them in the stout wooden mortar boxes.

Rock chips shovelled into these mills were soon reduced to powder, releasing the gold particles which had been disseminated through the quartz. Water passing over the mortar box carried the powder over sacking, where the gold, being heavier, was inclined to be trapped between the threads of the rough cloth. Every now and then the sacking would be washed out and the product panned to recover the gold.

The runoff from the mill would pass through several settling ponds which were periodically dug out and put into concrete cyanide tanks, where a solution of potassium cyanide would be poured over it. This dissolved the gold. This gold solution next went through tanks lined with zinc shavings, causing the gold to be deposited from the solution as a black powder, which after being removed and melted in a mud-walled charcoal furnace yielded bars of gold measuring around 15cm by 10cm by 1cm.

This modern Korean gold extraction process brought to mind a white quartz ring, once possessed by my grandfather, but now owned by a descendent. It is a good example of the old Korean gold extraction process. Gold in quartz or in a river deposit is rarely visible, yet those were the only sources of Korean gold before the establishment of the OCM.

What the Koreans learned from contact with American miners was evident at Eum Chum Khol, which until my father and his friends bought it was a native run mine where everyone except the Korean owner had been doing very well. The most advanced methods and machines were to be found at the OCM as they had the capital to import the latest equipment and techniques from America. In contrast to the original Korean methods, those used in Eum Chum Khol in the 1930s were positively high-tech.

Despite the improved mining methods in these remote regions, comparable advancements in transport and medicine had not reached the area, even though modern hospitals of Japanese and missionary origin were available in the cities.

Transport in and out of the region was on men's backs or by pony. For personal transport, you could hire coolies to haul you over the hills on a carrying chair, although if you were in a hurry you walked!

Diseases were still believed to be caused by evil spirits, requiring a *mudong* – a female witch doctor – to contact the spirits causing the disease. One day at the mine we observed a garishly dressed *mudong* accompanied by a small boy carrying and beating a huge hour-glass shaped drum, walking over the mine bridge and up Rose Quartz Valley to a patient's house.

On a previous mine visit my mother had observed the whole procedure. Following the *mudong* at a distance she saw that there were straw, paper and red rags fastened to bushes on the way up the valley, for these, especially red and silver, were said to be feared by evil spirits.

Outside the patient's house all manner of foodstuffs were piled such as garishly coloured cakes and persimmons. On entering the house the *mudong* examined the patient then flung a knife through the open door. Stepping outside she observed that its point was towards the house, which indicated to her that the evil spirits were still present. So she began scratching on a basket to attract their attention. Then she beckoned the spirits to her and listened to their message, nodding violently to indicate she understood.

Then she looked up for payment, which was extracted from the family and friends. Making a gesture to the drummer-boy, who started beating his drum harder, she held out her hand for more money and when she felt sufficiently remunerated she receded into a trance-like state. With snatching gestures she began a dance, becoming ever more frantic. She was shouting and screaming. With a crescendo of drumming she leap into the air, then fell flat in a heap as if dead.

The drumming ceased.

The evil spirits had departed, at least to the belief of the onlookers, so they all set about eating the cakes laid out for the evil spirits! Incidently, the word *mudong* means 'deceiving crowd', which just about sums up the quality of this 'medical' practice!

* * * *

One day, while I was sitting on the edge of the *malu*, typing a letter to relatives in England, a Korean miner came by on his way to the mine office. He looked at me and the thing on my knees with great intrigue, as he had never seen its like before. He probably concluded that the *sayan sarum* (foreigner) was playing some kind of musical instrument as it made a clicking sound and at intervals a bell sounded. It was in fact my Underwood portable typewriter, which I mentioned when describing my trip across Canada.

Another curious sound-making device was even more puzzling to the natives of Eum Chum Khol, where the delights of electricity were unknown and recent advances in lighting were limited to paraffin (kerosene) lamps, or the miners' carbide lamps. So when a contraption consisting of two boxes connected by what appeared to be a rope was unloaded from a pony, nobody had the slightest idea what it was, but another miner passing at night was amazed to hear voices coming out of one of the boxes! This was in fact our Emerson portable radio. At that time Japanese battery technology was not what it has become: the batteries were as big as the radio and it took a pony to carry them!

Having seen the mining methods of the Silver Working Valley and the modern methods of the OCM in far northern Korea I had an idea of what I needed to learn to be able to run this mine in the future. So we returned to Seoul and our home on the mountainside.

14

Holidays In The North

On return to Dilkusha we were approaching the rainy season, traditionally a time for our family to escape the damp heat and move north with some of the servants and at least one of our dogs to our summer house at Wonsan Beach. Before leaving we removed the stoves from Dilkusha's rooms and added screens to the windows.

Having packed our swimming suits and summer clothes we headed north by train, this time past Sambo-kyo on up to Wonsan. A taxi from the railway station took us to the Forty Li of Shining Sands (see Chapter 3).

The Japanese name for this north-eastern port city was Gensan, meaning 'Beginning Mountain'. As the Koreans and Japanese at that time used Chinese characters for writing – pronouncing them differently, but yielding the same meaning – a few names were pronounced slightly differently.

There is one great advantage of Chinese, complex though it is – you don't have to know the local language to determine the meaning of a character. A case in point was when our friend Chris Hupfer was coming up to our summer house. Finding that a Korean gentleman whom he asked the way didn't know Japanese, and Chris didn't speak Korean, he took a stick and drew the Chinese characters of his question in the earth at the side of the road. The Korean replied likewise and they both understood each other! So Chris was able to make his way to our summer home.

The chief sport at the beach was swimming, diving off a hired Korean junk. Sometimes people would take an outboard driven boat out to Bamboo Island for a picnic.

After some time at the beach, the Japanese government announced that they had arranged to buy the beach and that they would help the Wonsan Beach Association, which owned it, to get some other beach land further south. They wanted the place for an airfield and gave us land in what later turned out to be South Korea. It was called Whashinpo, in English this was Flower Ferry Lake. There was a pine forest between a large lake and the seashore with a small island about a mile offshore, in a region surrounded by hills. A vast improvement for us over Wonsan Beach.

Whashinpo, "Flower Ferry Lake, on the shore of the Eastern Sea,(Sea of Japan) South Korea.

At the end of the rainy season the lake overflowed into the sea just beyond the lake shore, bringing countless fish with it, resulting in a heyday for local fishermen.

Later in the autumn the Wonsan Beach Association met at Whashinpo and lots were drawn for the new building sites. The house lots had been marked off with the locations and numbers. People could go around and see which ones they liked, then when their names were drawn they could ask for the ones they had picked out as their favourites.

Mum had signed MLT/DV on the markers of the lot she chose. MLT stood for Mary Linley Taylor, DV stood for a Latin expression, Deo volonte, commonly used in England at the time to mean 'God willing'. It completely bypassed the Americans as everyone else thought that the lot had already been assigned, so they didn't ask for it and we got Mum's chosen site!

Provision was made to ship the dismantled houses (from Wonsan) by sea or railway to the new site. At the end of the summer season we had packed up, the house was dismantled, shipped south and, when lots had been chosen, reconstructed. The house now faced Flower Ferry Lake, which was perhaps 20 yards in front of it. About 200 yards to the north-west lay a nice sandy beach and the sea. The land sloped up in the steps of former rice fields to the coastal hills behind the house. The land was very fertile there so it seemed like a good spot to plant our vegetable garden.

Most of the other house sites were on sand. Our house was reconstructed by Moksu, our Chinese carpenter. We addressed him by this Korean word for carpenter as no one seemed to know his Chinese name.

At Wonsan, the house had been given a name – The Haven – in the English fashion. But Mum decided to re-name it Eight Bells, which on a ship signifies meal time, thus implying that friends were always welcome. Between the cemented stone pillars either side of the entrance to the house we spelled out its name with water worn stones set into cement.

Early in the summer season of 1938 Mum and I, along with Nam Do (our Korean cook) and Moksu, went to the house to prepare for the coming summer. Essentially the downstairs was a large L-shaped room, the base of the L being the living area and the upright being the dining area, which faced the lake. The living area faced the more distant sea. There had been a downstairs bedroom in the middle of the L, but Mum and I had the carpenter move the wall so it became too small for a bedroom but big enough for a changing room for swimming.

Beyond this little room was the kitchen and next to it the bathroom, complete with wooden Japanese bath tub and the usual convenience similar to that at Wonsan. An enclosed shed beyond the kitchen contained a hand-operated force pump which proved its use later on.

When we were preparing to depart from Wonsan we had dismantled the fireplace, the curving mantlepiece and hearth, which was in a half-circle of radiating bricks, and carefully numbered each piece for re-assembly. However, at Wha Shin Po we found a nearby beach with a lot of nicely water-worn stones and had them brought by a coolie on a *jiggy*. We built a new fireplace with them in the same radiating pattern of the original brick fireplace and hearth.

While the fireplace was being constructed with Mum, myself and Nam Do on the inside, a Korean contractor was building the chimney on the outside. Neither party really knew what the other group was doing. Eventually we puzzled out how to get the smoke up the chimney instead of into the room.

While working on the fireplace one night I started feeling bitterly cold, despite the warm weather. Then things reversed and I developed a considerable fever. It was the chills and fever of malaria, which the resident Dr Demaree confirmed. The bouts of chills and fever came and went so there were periods when I was totally lacking in energy and others when I was quite well. Being a cheerful soul, the doctor told me I might have it on and off for 20 years! Thanks to subsequently developed drugs this did not prove to be the case. Strangely, years later, malaria proved to be a blessing in disguise.

Returning to the chimney trials: once we got the fire going we observed flames shooting out of the top of the chimney, where the remaining wood left by the contractor had caught fire! Korean houses at that time often had chimneys made of wood or even straw sacking. But that was due to their sub-floor heating which was really far more efficient than ours, causing the smoke to be quite cool when emitted from their short chimneys. The force pump enabled us to spray water on the tar paper roof until the fire eventually burned out the remains of the old chimney form.

The entire second floor of the house was used as a bedroom. Formerly, the downstairs bedroom was taken over by my father who slept in late so everyone had to tip-toe around for much of the day. Reducing this room to changing-room size moved Dad upstairs. We used the built-in bunks downstairs for beds at night and couches during the day. This was a great improvement for Mum and I.

In front of the house a grove of pine trees along the lake

shore had a nice natural opening, allowing a view of the lake and the distant mountains on its far side. This opening had been improved by a little moonlight trimming near the trees' roots, which were then covered with earth. The Japanese authorities were rather fussy about tree-cutting without permits, but they were far away.

The house, located at the foot of a valley with a view from its side windows to the sea, had a lake view to the front. The coastal mountains rose above the old paddy fields behind the house. We used both the lake and the sea for swimming. I recall one time when the sea was quite rough and we used the incoming waves to bring us in, then stood firm in the shallow water and waited for the next waves to push us ashore. When things were finished in refurnishing the house at the end of summer, I went with Dr Demaree to his house alongside his hospital in Wonsan where he treated me with quinine, at that time the standard drug to combat my intermittent bouts of fever.

Mum and the servants returned to Seoul for the winter. When Dr Demaree had stabilized my condition, I too took the train south. However, in the following spring, 1939, malaria returned and our family doctor, Dr George Rue in Seoul, sent me to his nicely situated Seventh Day Adventist Hospital out in the delightful country region beyond Tongdaemun (or in Japanese Todaimon) – Seoul's Great East Gate. This was a pleasant contrast to the rather crowded city area of the Presbyterian Severance Hospital next to the railway station and Nandaemun (Nandaimon, in Japanese) – the Great South Gate of the city.

Here I was treated with a new drug called Atabrin which stopped the disease and left me with no more malarial symptoms for three years, until I was a US soldier on Guadalcanal in the Solomon Islands of the South Pacific.

Some time after recovering in Seoul, Dad suggested that I take about 100 runners from our strawberry beds in Dilkusha's garden and plant them in the soil beside the Whashinpo house. So going with Nam Do and Moksu I went to Whashinpo somewhat ahead of the usual summer migration and planted them along with okra, aubergine (eggplant), potatoes, lettuce and the like which thrived there. Later, after going to college in California, I heard from Dad that the strawberries did so well that three berries would fill a saucer!

Besides improving the fresh vegetable supply, we also took a remarkable device that proved useful for lighting inside the house and for fishing at night. This was a carbide lamp of the same type used at the mine, but unlike the miners' headlamps this was an upright standing lamp for room illumination. Basically a vertical cylinder containing chunks of calcium carbide, with a smaller water container on top with a valve to control the water flow. A metal pipe brought the gas, released by the water to a pair of gas jets at the end of the pipe. When lit they formed a brilliant white u-shaped flame, much brighter than a Coleman petrol (gasoline) lantern. Also the lamp needed neither pumping nor mantles.

While we were there we saw the local Koreans walking around the lake one night catching fish in a rather novel manner. One man carried a wire basket of blazing pine sticks on the end of a pole while the others, armed with tridents, were spearing fish revealed by the fire.

These fish, which were rather like sole, lay quite still and were thus an easy mark. We, using the carbide lamp and bamboo poles with a nail at the end, duplicated their work and caught 86 fish in two hours.

One day, walking on the beach after a storm at sea, I saw a long and somewhat straight tree trunk with a right-angled bend near one end, then another bend further on that brought the trunk back to its original direction. A few weeks later we saw in the nearby Korean village a new house which had used the double-angled trunk as part of the front of the house. The natives, lacking the machines to shape the tree trunk, just shaped the house to fit the trunk.

Many years later, when I had become a teacher in California, I used this as an example to show why it was so necessary in our much more advanced world to learn mathematics and learn to do things accurately, for you might build a house in Korea with crooked logs, but you couldn't build planes with crooked wings in America and expect them to fly.

At one time while at Whashinpo with Dad, a Korean miner came to tell him of an outcrop of potential gold-bearing ore which had been found near the opposite side of the lake. So, as Dad was not well enough to go, I walked for miles around the lake shore with the miner, collected samples and returned to Dad to have them assayed for gold content.

Whashinpo was a considerable distance from any large town, so the missionaries asked the Chinese owner of Steward's Grocery Shop in Seoul (he had once been a steward on a ship), who supplied all sorts of imported foreign food products from America, England, Australia and Japan, to build a branch at the beach – a good deal for customers and the store owner, as he had no competitors! It was handy for us as it was only a few hundred yards from our house.

There was a railway station at the north end of the lake. When coming to Whashinpo at the start of the summer we walked around the edge of the lake to our house. If we were going away for the day we would paddle our canoe to the station, pull it ashore and leave it there. On return we could paddle it and accrued luggage back to the house. The dogs preferred running along the shore, keeping pace with us – they looked very bored if we made them sit in the boat.

Sometimes we would walk through the nearby Korean farming village at the south end of the lake, consisting of a few houses. We would continue on up a trail through the coastal ranges of hills to a rocky beach, which proved to be the source of the pretty water-worn stones that we had used for the fireplace and other construction at Eight Bells.

This was my last summer at Whashinpo and I was malaria free. We had a friend from China staying with us who before arriving had learned that "the balloon had gone up", as was the expression of the times. The war in Europe had started. And the spread of that war to Asia and the Pacific in time ended those pacific days for us and our life in Asia.

After our friend had returned to China, Mum and I were alone at Whashinpo. The deciduous trees on the hillsides behind us were losing their leaves in the autumn and Dad, who had returned Seoul, was away on a business trip. So instead of returning to Seoul, via Wonsan, we decided to take a few days to walk through Kumkansang, the Diamond Mountains, much as my parents had done a couple of decades earlier.

We took the train to Changjon, beside the sea, at the entrance to the inner reaches of these remarkable mountains. Seeing them in pictures, with so many unusual, dramatically pointed peaks, one was apt to think that artists had been carried away with vivid imaginations.

In those days there was no road or rail route into the mountains, you either walked or employed the services of coolies with a carrying chair. We walked.

During the Japanese rule of Korea the region was called the Kongo San, the Anglicized version of the Japanese name for the mountains. And the sea coast was known as the Umikongo, or Seakongo.

Knowing, as we thought, in those far off days of peace 68 years ago, as I write this, that we could always return to the Umikongo later, we concentrated on the route into the Uchikongo (Inner Diamond Mountains). That complacent idea was changed by subsequent events, so here is how my mother described the journey in her prior trip to the region, from *Chain of Amber*:

"We explored the [seashore region of] Kumkansang, as [the mountains] are called. Here it looked as though an entire range had slipped into the ocean. The peaks which had emerged had been worn by the sea into fantastic shapes of Buddhas and seals and the basalt tips which had broken from the mainland stood like Corinthian pillars, tufted with pine trees, washed by lashing turquoise water, and inhabited by bird colonies. Here and there, where one had fallen from the rest, tremendous 80-foot-tall caves were exposed with arms of the sea stretching back far into their depths.

"We hired a fishing junk and the boatman took us to an island. We landed on the flat surface left by the broken pillars and it was like a tessellated pavement of six sided tiles. The cracks were filled with ruby-red sea anemones. It was hot to the feet so we plunged in and swam about. While Bruce went round the island I swam up the dark aisle of the cave. The sea boomed in it like a distant organ but my poetic mood was sharply broken when I felt a clammy body clinging to the full length of my own. Terrified I turned and struggled back to the opening, which looked so far away. When I reached it, the creature slid free of me and floated helplessly out to sea. It was an enormous jellyfish, like a parachute trailing yards of iridescent rainbow-coloured tentacles behind it."

My mother and I spent a night in a more or less Western-style hotel owned by a Korean, and the next day we started our walk through the mountains. We could find no local or Japanese name for some of the interesting places we stopped at so just made up some of our own.

In Changjon we found a shop selling guide books in several languages, including one in Japanese and English which gave the names and legends connected to each site. Each place in the guide book corresponded to places in the mountains bearing official sign posts with identical signs to those in the book. These were in Kanji, Chinese characters used in Japanese writing. Though neither of us were conversant in Kanji at that time we could compare the signs on the sites with those in the book to figure out where we were, then read the English explanation.

There were many fantastic jagged peaks and tall thin spires of rock, which on reflection I think must have been ancient weathered basalt columns. At one such place we climbed up and found a wide, flat spot with enough room for both of us to sit together for a picnic lunch.

As often happens when packing in a strange place, some

things get mixed up. And so it had happened to us. We found that I had the sandwiches and Mum had my spare rock hammer, which was considerably heavier. I had wondered where it was, and Mum had wondered why the lunch was so heavy! I was told to carry my own extra baggage in future.

While we ate our sandwiches we looked at our dual-language guide book to find that our particular spire resembled a devil, but when Mum painted its picture it looked like a bishop. Beauty is in the eye of the beholder.

Walking on from there we climbed up a narrow opening through the rocks, assisted by some iron rungs driven into the rock wall. We came out into a flat expanse beneath a sheer vertical rock wall extending hundreds of feet upwards. Down one side of this rock face thundered a great waterfall into a swirling pool. To one side, and many yards from the waterfall, was a Korean pavilion with a roof but no sides where one could sit and enjoy the view of the Nine Dragon Pool (so our trusty guide book informed us). It went on to tell us of the legend associated with these falls and pool, which goes like this:

When the Buddhist monks came from India about 1,400 years ago, and decided that this was an ideal area to introduce Buddhism, they rested for a while under a tree which was near a rocky pool in a river. However, the pool was occupied by nine dragons who informed the monks that this was their territory and told them to be gone. To prove their point, the dragons whipped up a storm which blew the tree away. The monks, unmoved, wrote something on a piece of paper and cast it into the pool, which became boiling hot. The dragons jumped into a river with eight pools – the ninth one was swept over the falls and has been there ever since, kept by the swirling water at the base of the Nine Dragon Falls.

If you have sufficient Buddhist faith you could see him to that day. I didn't, but then I am not a Buddhist.

From there we went on to a place where there was said to be a giant statue of Buddha. We looked in every direction without seeing anything. Then, gazing behind us, we found the entire cliff had a 60-foot statue of Buddha carved into it!

As it was getting towards evening, we decided to push on to Pirobong, the topmost peak of the Diamond Mountains, at whose foot there was a large Japanese hotel, which resembled the ski lodge at Sambo Kyo (Medicine Spring) 12 miles from our gold mine. It had a large dormitory room, a section with traditional Japanese hotel rooms and a public bathroom. We rented one of the Japanese rooms for a couple of nights.

Our room had the usual *tatami* woven straw mat floors with cushions to sit on and futons to sleep on or under. It had large sliding windows and sliding *shoji* screens that divided us from the passage that led to the bathroom and the rest of the hotel.

It was a clean, cozy room. I could feel really at home in such a place – a vast improvement over the Korean hotels of prior experience. Delightful Japanese meals were even brought to our room.

Visits to the bathroom were quite different to our Western traditions. There was a large pool of warm water, like a small swimming pool. And over to one side there were benches where you could sit to disrobe and leave your clothes. There were wooden tubs that you could fill from the pool, wash yourself off, then rinse yourself and get into the pool for a nice hot soak.

We practiced our Western customs of one person of each sex at a time in the room. But the Japanese think nothing of mixed-sex nude bathing! Mum had a bit of a culture shock on her honeymoon in the bathroom of a Japanese hotel: she was in the pool, *sans* clothes of course, when in walked a Japanese gentleman and his family and insisted on introducing them to her, all nude!

The following day we had a lovely view of row after descending row of the mountain ranges below us extending down to the Eastern Sea, as the Koreans call the Sea of Japan. After breakfast we walked down to the temple beneath the giant Buddha.

Our guide book directed us to what I will call the Wailing Stream, for lack of its real name. It made a curious sound which the Koreans said sounded like a person wailing the death of someone.

Coming to the place in the book we found two large boulders beside the stream. One had three beautifully carved images of Buddha in bas-relief, the other had 100 rather poorly carved images.

The legend connected to this site told of a teacher and a priest, both students of Buddhism, who were constantly contending with each other as to who knew the most about the subject. To settle the argument once and for all, one challenged the other to take his pick – either carve a hundred small bas-reliefs of Buddha on the nearby rocks, or three large ones. An independent judge would decide which was the best.

The priest carved the three large images and was judged the best. The teacher carved 100 small ones of distinctly inferior quality. He committed suicide and the stream has been wailing for him ever since, believe it or not.

In the afternoon, after another picnic lunch, we walked upstream to the Maiyokodai or the Mirror Rock Pool, where there was a tall, solid rock shaped rather like an arch, in front of which was a calm pool that reflected the rock. It was said that a man from South Korea had died and descended to Buddhist Hell where the King of Hell stood on a rock and looked into a mirror to see all the sins he had committed. But he saw that the man was not supposed to die just yet, and sent him back to his family.

On returning to earth the man decided to make a pilgrimage to the Diamond Mountains. When he reached the Maiyokodai it looked to him like a replica of the scene in Hell. And what was more there were two holes behind the rock – one just like that which led to Yellow Snake Hell, where sinners were sent for 5,000 years, and another resembling that which led to Red Snake Hell, where really evil sinners 'did time' for 10,000 years.

Following our walk we returned to our mountain top hotel for one last night. Taking advantage of the public telegraph available in the hotel we sent a message informing Dad we would return the next day. There were often mix-ups in telegraphs due to the lack of English knowledge among the operators, such as when a missionary named Hall was informed that a correspondent would see him in Hell!

When we were descending the path to the valley below, we gazed at a little hermitage temple built on a cliff ledge. It was said that the first hermit was inspired by Kwanin, Goddess of Mercy, to build his hermitage there. I have a painting of this by Mum in Oriental style hanging on my wall as I write.

Further down the path we saw a Japanese artist painting the scene in black and white on a small booklet. He had a bamboo-handled brush, attached by a cord to a much wider section of bamboo with a lid to hold a cloth soaked in ink.

Eventually we reached the valley floor and came to a considerable group of temple buildings with characteristic up-turned roof corners. Passing Changansa Temple, the Temple Of Eternal Rest, we could see in the flickering votive lights the golden glow of huge Buddha images and the chanting, if I recall it correctly, of: "*Omne pade mun, oh thou jewel in the heart of the lotus.*"

As we left the temple, Mum remarked that over the coming years we would be able to repeatedly return to this wonderful region of fantastic mountains, temples and fanciful stories.

Such are the changes and chances of this mortal life. Though each of us did individually return at different times to South Korea, neither of us ever returned to this land of wonder in the North.

We walked to the local train station and caught the little electric train back to Seoul, returning again to Dilkusha, where we were greeted by the third member of our Alsatian family, Bong, our resident one-dog police force, whose presence discouraged intruders. And we were in due course allowed one last Christmas together in Seoul.

* * * *

Thanks to our family enthusiast, Mum's youngest sister Una, one more fantastic adventure awaited us.

In January 1940 Una had a week's holiday from her job with

Standard Oil, coinciding with the big New Year's holiday of the Japanese. So making contact with the local missionaries we were able to book rooms in a missionary compound in Peking (Beijing), China, and take the day-and-a-half long train trip on the Japanese South Manchurian Railway to the northern capital of what had been called the Middle Kingdom. Peking is now pronounced Beijing, though its name is still written in the Chinese characters for 'northern capital'.

We left Seoul Station in the evening, and awoke in our sleepers the next day to find ourselves travelling along a featureless mud-coloured plain, occasionally crossing bridges with guard posts at each end, staffed by Japanese soldiers. Here and there we passed houses built in the form of a square with high walls all round, and a central garden area in the middle, another indication of a lawless land where houses had to be built as fortresses. One also occasionally saw de-railed locomotives lying on their sides in the earth beside the tracks. Chinese bandits made transportation in Japanese-controlled Manchuria somewhat hazardous.

The train stopped at Tiensin, China, while I was in the dining car. An English-speaking Chinese gentleman came in. Not knowing Japanese he couldn't make himself understood, but I, a foreigner in his land, was able to translate for him, as my knowledge of Japanese was passable at that time.

Most of the houses we saw in Peking were built on that same 'fortress' plan: high walls all round a confined single entrance which could be closed by a lofty gate. Rooms were built inside the high walls and the central open area might contain a garden.

During our week in Peking we were each able to get our

own rickshaw coolies for $30 Mex each, to take us anywhere we wanted to go during the week. (China had been using Mexican currency for some time, commonly referred to as dollars Mex.)

There was a curious exchange rate difference between US dollars, Chinese dollars Mex and Japanese yen. In Korea 1 US dollar got you 4 yen, but in Peking 1 US dollar was worth 40 dollars Mex. One dollar Mex was equivalent to 1 yen, so missionaries paid in US dollars travelled to Peking to change their dollars into dollars Mex, then into yen, having a nice trip and coming back with more money than they started with.

So many of the houses and buildings had tall walls surrounding them that there were many rather dark roadways between buildings. Various streets were the exclusive domain of shops catering to certain crafts. For example, one street was devoted to cloisonné work, where brass bowls, jars and the like would have thin strips of brass soldered to their outsides, often in the shape of leaves or flowers. Coloured powders were added to the brass, which was fired in a kiln to fuse the powders in the desired shape. These were then ground flat and polished, before the metal was gold plated and finely polished again.

Other products such as trees made with semi-precious stones were obtainable in another specialist street, and so on.

There was a multitude of signs in Chinese characters around the streets, as one would expect, although now and then one came across attempts at English, which certainly attracted attention. One such sign read: "*Glass Eyes and False Teeth Installed by the Latest Methodists.*"

Leading to two of Peking's famous temples – the Lama Temple and the Temple of Heaven – there were three doors, two with steps enabling bearers to carry the Emperor up the elaborately carved central Spirit Way, reserved for him and the spirits entering the temple.

Although the Japanese controlled Peking, fighting with the Chinese continued around nearby sections of the Great Wall, so we were unfortunately unable to pay a visit.

The Japanese military liked to show their self-importance in the city by driving their trucks through foreign settlements well in excess of the speed limit. This was effectively countered by notices at the entrances warning: "Motorists are warned of bumps in the road."

The speeding Japanese soon found they were banging their heads on the roofs of their trucks and decided to slow down.

Before our week was up we had to go to the Manchukuo Consulate and waste a morning getting a one-way visa to pass through that puppet kingdom. None had been required for the first trip through their territory. But the Japanese had installed Henry Pu Yi as the Emperor of Manchukuo – the land of the Manchus. In reality it was the land of the Japanese, with themselves as top dogs and the Manchus at the bottom, just as was the case for Korea, although the Koreans had lost even the pretence of a puppet king.

One member of the Taylor tribe did well out of Henry Pu Yi's establishment as Emperor. Dad's brother Bill showed up with a pair of huge Chinese urns as a gift for him and got an order, it was reported, for 2,000 General Motors trucks!

* * * *

Shortly after our return home to Seoul I celebrated my 21st birthday. It was 28 February 1940 and, according to the laws of that time, I had attained adulthood. I was given a trip to California and monthly funds to enable me to start studying to be a mining engineer, with the intention to return with a degree in mining, in due course to take over from Dad and run the family business.

Mum took me into the garden and pointed out that I would always have this and all the family estates to come back to. Curiously, I felt in my own mind that I would never see it Again, but I did not mention it. I never did see it again as I knew it, nor did I ever possess it.

15

Eastwards To The West

The best laid schemes o' mice an' men
Gang aft agley
Robert Burns, To A Mouse

In the normal course of events, I would inherit a goodly heritage consisting of Dilkusha with its 12-acre garden, W W Taylor & Co's four-storey office building in a good downtown location, part ownership of the Gold Mine at Eum Chum Khol in North Korea, and our summer house, Eight Bells, at Whashinpo on the shores of the Eastern Sea (Sea of Japan).

I thought to myself that my chosen career was to be in Chosen – Korea – to pursue gold mining. The Japanese rulers of Korea also thought they had everything nicely sewn up. Yet the passage of five years utterly changed both our plans.

* * * *

And so in 1940 the day came for me to take the train to Busan (Fusan), the ferry to Shimonoseki, the train to Yokohama and in due course the *Kokusai Maru*, with large *hino maru* (Japanese rising sun flags) painted on its sides, for a two-week voyage to San Pedro, California.

Mrs. Main, who had also been born in Korea of American

missionary parents, met me and took me to her house near San Diego for a few days, then I took a train to Oakland and spent a few days with my father's sister, my Aunt Olive in Alameda. She helped me sign up for summer school at the University of California. After six weeks there I was advised to go to the College of Marin to make up some courses. I spent a year in Kentfield at that delightful little college in the beautiful wooded country region beneath Mount Tamalpais.

However, when it came time to register for the next year, another registration took priority. I had to register for the draft. War in Europe looked like engulfing America too, and the armed forces were being expanded. Draftees were being shipped for training to Oklahoma, which I didn't think was OK. So instead, by volunteering for four years in the Regular Army, I was able to choose the Engineers in Hawaii.

In a few weeks I was sent back across the Pacific to Oahu, in the Hawaiian Islands, which I had last glimpsed just before my sixth birthday. We were initially stationed at the nice airy Schofield Barracks in the Head Quarters Company of the 65th Engineers, but were soon encamped in tents during our six weeks of basic training, learning to be soldiers and Army engineers. Of course this was not utterly new to me with my past experience in the British Officers Training Corps and an American Military Academy.

Basic training finished on Friday 5 December 1941, and the next day I left for Honolulu to see Rev and Mrs. Henry Appenzeller, former Methodist missionaries in Seoul, as well as their daughter Carol, who had attended the Seoul Foreign School with Joyce Phipps, daughter of our best friends in Seoul, Gerald and Aline Phipps, the British Consul General and his wife.

We didn't have to get up too early the following day, being a Sunday, and were taking it easy when planes started flying overhead.

"Why on Sunday?" we wondered.

Someone said: "Oh, it's the Air Force, they never do things when anyone else does them."

It was *an* Air Force alright, but not ours! I looked out and saw the familiar red suns, the *hino maru* on the sides and wings of the planes. It was the Japanese Naval Air Force attacking Henderson Air Field – right next to us.

The loud-speaker on the wall suddenly barked: "Alert! Everyone out and bring your rifles."

It was lucky they had not been locked in their racks the night before after use on the rifle range.

Reaching the ground floor we were handed bandoleers holding five-round clips for Springfield rifles and empty steel clips for our semi-automatic Garand rifles for eight rounds per clip. We quickly reloaded the rounds into the steel clips so we could use our rapid-firing rifles. I drew a bead on an incoming plane and was tracking it in my sights. I slowly began to squeeze the trigger when it flapped its wings! It was a seagull! I refrained, and that was the nearest I came to combat in my entire four years in the Army. Due to my knowledge of typing, radio, photography and Japanese I got a variety of non-combat jobs requiring those skills.

For most of a year on Oahu I used the first two of those skills and during that time saw the Appenzellers several times. I soon learned of a way of contacting my parents, now interned in Korea as 'enemy aliens'. Short-wave radio station KGEI in San Francisco would read 25-word messages over its Missionary Mail Bag programme, so I sent several messages to "Bruce and Mary, somewhere in the Orient," so as not to give the Japanese any idea of where they were. Our friends the Phipps and Bishop Cecil Cooper of the Anglican Cathedral of St Nicholas both had short-wave sets when I left Korea.

Before we left Oahu I had learned through my Aunt Una, who was working in New York with Standard Oil, that my parents had been repatriated and were now in Long Beach, California. I had their phone number so was able to phone them for a few minutes and mention that I had seen and said goodbye to the Appenzellers. My parents knew where they were, thus got the idea that I was going somewhere else. All out-going phone calls were censored, so I had been able to give my parents a hint that I was leaving Hawaii.

* * * *

I sailed with the Engineers to places unknown, and wound up on Guadalcanal, in the Soloman Islands.

During the journey some amateur astronomers on board the troopship were able to figure out the direction and our changing locations across the Pacific as we approached Noumea, New Caledonia. Simple compasses gave the direction, the height of the North Star gave us the latitude and the time on the ship's clocks gave us the longitude. At

Noumea we were told we were heading for Guadalcanal and might have to fight our way ashore.

However, we landed peacefully as the Marines had arrived and driven the Japanese troops inland. We pitched our six-man tents in a coconut grove. The Head Quarters Company Radio Section, which I was in, had nothing to do for at least three weeks as the radios had not been landed with us. There was a wrecked Higgins boat (landing craft) with its landing ramp down facing the sea near our camp so we often used it to go for a swim.

We had landed just before Christmas and on Christmas Day attended holy communion conducted by an Episcopal chaplain, using the bonnet (hood) of his Jeep as an altar.

My experiences at Whashinpo and the Seventh Day Adventist Hospital in Seoul – and the local mosquitoes – combined to further my good life in the Army. I got malaria for the sixth time. So I went to the medical tent, told them my malarial history and asked for a heavy dose of Atabrin, as that had cured my fifth bout of the fever.

They put me straight onto an empty troopship which took me first to a Naval hospital in the New Hebrides. One of the other soldiers on that ship was a fellow geology student who had been the same class of nine students at the College of Marin!

We made a few stops at islands, including Fiji, then transferred to a Matson liner back to San Francisco's Letterman Hospital in the Presidio Army Base. While I was there another soldier showed a group of us some photos he had picked up on Guadalcanal, left by the retreating Japanese

Army. I saw a picture taken outside the Diamond Mountain hotel, and another on the pine-covered slope below Mount Yangwhasan near Dilkusha!

When we first reached the Presidio I borrowed a nickel (five cents) to dial the telephone operator and make a collect call to my parents in Long Beach.

My father

My Mother

Mum promptly came up to see me. She talked to the chaplain who in turn got me a month's leave, so I was able to spend most of that time with Mum and Dad.

Before returning to the base I went to the College of Marin to talk to my friendly advisor. While we were chatting a student came up to ask him to sign a paper. The advisor asked if I knew who the student was. I had no idea. He said that student was the brother of the soldier who had been in my geology class!

On return to my new assignment in the headquarters of A Company at the Presidio, the first order I picked up assigned me to the military police guard unit at Tule Lake Relocation Centre in far northern California, not far from the Oregon border, in a dry lake bed just south of Klamath Falls, Oregon.

When on Guadalcanal I had read in *Yank*, the Army newspaper, that the Army was seeking GIs who knew Japanese, so when I was on leave I recovered a Japanese language textbook that I had used in Korea and took it with me. I told everyone that Japanese was my second language and studied the book daily. It paid off in the end.

Military Intelligence sent a man to recruit Japanese-Americans who were interned in the Relocation Centre. Luckily for me he had a cold and was advised to go to the guard unit where a doctor told him I spoke Japanese. When he interviewed me he asked if I could read the language. I read a page of the text I had been studying. He said it was good enough and I could expect to hear from his commanding officer. It turned out that this officer knew my father as they had been repatriated from Japan on the same ship!

Shortly thereafter I was transferred to the Military Intelligence Japanese Language School, at the University of Michigan, for a year.

During that time I travelled to New York to see my mother's sisters – my Aunt Una, Aunt Betty and her husband, my Uncle Maurice – and to Detroit to see friends of theirs. At the end of each semester we got 10 days' academic leave, plus a couple of three-day passes, and thanks to a member of A Company who had worked for the Santa Fe Railroad we were all able to get express train tickets at reduced prices, so during that year I saw Mum and Dad three times in Long Beach.

* * * *

I was transferred again towards the end of the war to the 144 MP PWP Co (Military Police Prisoner-of-War Processing Company) as an interpreter-cum-photographer. We were to take photos, finger prints and make records of prisoners of war, but few Japanese, if any, would surrender – they preferred suicide. They only surrendered when the Emperor ordered them to do so after the dropping of the atomic bombs.

Until that happened 144 MP PWP Co had a nice vacation at Army expense, with tours from New Guinea to Australia and then the Philippines. When the Japanese surrendered it looked as though we would be there for a decade.

However, prior Army adventures had earned me many points for early discharge and I was returned to San Pedro, California, for discharge four years, two months and two days after I signed up.

I headed straight for the Huntington Hotel on palm tree-lined East Ocean Boulevard, Long Beach, where my parents had an ocean-front apartment.

PART III

16

Muntata!

Muntata! **Shut the door! World** War II and the Korean War had shut the door on the Taylor family's activity in Korea.

Mining or the import-export business was out of the question so I sought a different profession. My parents had been doing war work while marking time until they could return to Korea. On settling in Long Beach they had re-established contact with their friends the Phipps, now retired in Seaford, England. One Christmas they sent a family photo to us with an accompanying letter from Aline Phipps, which said: "Last night Joyce dreamed that she met Bruce's elder brother."

I, who had always told my mother that I wanted to marry an English girl, took advantage and wrote to Joyce about her dream saying I was my elder brother, for I was an only child.

A steady stream of letters ensued in both directions and I also managed a trans-Atlantic phone call. That cost me a week's pay of my factory job, but it was worth it!

I worked in sundry jobs until I could return to college classes at Long Beach City College. I met some interesting teachers there. One, who had been educated in New York, had a low opinion of the Californian concept of education called progressive education for democracy. He regarded it as rather ineffective. Subsequent experience with it led me to the same conclusion.

Another instructor gave me the idea of buying land and building a house, which I designed and received a building department permit to construct.

But while laying out the stakes prior to construction, Dad died of a heart attack. His brother Bill, who was working in the American Military Government of Korea, had recently told him that he was to be appointed head of the Department of Mines, but his sudden death ended that.

Mum immediately started trying to get to Korea to carry out his last wishes. If he died before returning to Korea he wanted to be buried beside his father, George Alexander Taylor, in the Yang Hwa Jin Foreigners' Cemetery in Seoul.

This seemed impossible. There was an airline and shipping strike on and visas were not being issued for Korea. But Mum did not know the meaning of 'impossible'. She ploughed ahead and in due course got permission to sail on a troopship to Japan, from where she got the go-ahead to go to Korea.

Meanwhile, Una, who had worked in New York with Standard Oil, had moved back to Japan with the company to help the Army with oil supplies. Her contacts in the Judge Advocate General's office gained permission for the two sisters to return to Korea and attend Dad's final funeral. They stayed with their friends the Underwoods, a famed missionary family, who had founded Chosen Christian College, which later became Yonsei University.

After a week in Seoul they had completed arrangements for Dad's last rites, gathered all their friends who had returned to Seoul, and with our good friend Father Charles Hunt of the Anglican Church officiating, buried my father's ashes next to his father George Alexander Taylor in the Yang Hwa Jin Foreigners' Cemetery.

Mum then had an interview with Dr Syngman Rhee, the first President of Korea, just before he was due to review the troops of the new Korean Army. She showed him documents that had been kept safe in the American Consulate since 1 March 1919, when my father's actions the day after my birth had saved the lives of many Koreans, including Syngman Rhee's parents.

Incredibly, Mum saved Dr Rhee's life by delaying him with this information, for just before he reached the troops a bomb planted by Communists exploded on the reviewing stand.

* * * *

Meanwhile, Aline Phipps, hearing that Mum would be in Korea at Christmas, had invited me to spend the holiday period with her family in Seaford. So I sold the land I had bought back to the man I bought it from, using the proceeds to buy a return bus ticket to New York and a ship berth to Liverpool, England. I spent Christmas at Brown Gables in Seaford, East Sussex, and became engaged to Joyce, saying I would return in a year or two to marry her.

Joyce Phipps on the Downs above Seaford, Sussex, England.

On our respective returns from Korea and England Mum and I made plans to move to northern California so I could continue my studies at the College of Marin. In the intervening time I spent a year in the Active Naval Reserve with night classes at college.

At the end of the year I transferred to the Inactive Naval Reserve, and registered my college credits with Marin. Then we loaded up our belonging into my $50 wonder – an old grey Dodge which we called The Whippet – and drove about 500 miles from Long Beach to Stinson Beach, in Marin County, California.

I spent a year at the college, first driving daily over Mount Tamalpais to classes, then resorting to the bus. I then received an honourable discharge from the Naval Reserve. An aptitude test at the college revealed that I would make a good teacher, so on graduation from the College of Marin with an Associate of Arts degree, I transferred to San Francisco State Teacher's College.

* * * *

An unexpected GI insurance bonus cheque enabled me to buy a return flight to England with my mother and marry Joyce Phipps in Seaford, the ceremony conducted by her brother John, a Church of England priest, on 1 July 1950. This day is now Canada Day, but Our Day wherever we are.

Wedding, Seaford, Sussex, England 1st July 1950
Bruce T.Taylor & Joyce Phipps.

We spent a month on honeymoon driving around in her father's car, which he kindly lent to us for the first fortnight. After that we took the train to Scotland to stay with some of Joyce's friends, then flew back to New York where a bus took us to California via Virginia, where we stayed for a week with friends of Joyce's parents who used to live in Japan.

Back on the west coast we started our married life in Stinson Beach before buying a house of our own in Corte Madera, Marin County, with Mum's help and a marriage allowance from the GI Bill for Veterans of World War II. Mum meanwhile bought a house across the valley in Larkspur with money from the sale of Dilkusha in Seoul.

For about six months Joyce had a job as a telephone operator in Larkspur, adding to the family finances, then later through her Aunt Jessie, in Seaford, she made contact with the manager of the Hong Kong Shanghai Bank in San Francisco and worked there for many years on a better pay scale.

I spent two years at San Francisco State College and in 1952 graduated with a BA and an Elementary Teaching Credential. I got a job for a year at the Novato School District, in Marin County, California, where I tried the progressive education method. It was a complete failure!

I then went to the Sausalito School District, in the same county, where their experiment with progressive education was also a failure. Many teachers left and new ones with firmer backgrounds were hired. The new principal – an ex-US Marine Corps Captain – set much stricter standards. My Military Police background was considered an asset.

For the next six years – 1953 to 1959 – I taught seventh grade at the Sausalito School District with success, using the firm but fair methods of my prep school, St Pirans. I even asked for the students other teachers couldn't stand. As a result I got a class of bright, but previously bored students, turned off by the same low expectations of the previous method. During my last term there, a young African American in a Marine Corps Captain's uniform, with two silver bars indicating his rank, came into my room and said: "You gave me these silver bars, for you taught me how to study."

* * * *

Five years after our marriage, our son Peter Maclean joined the family, on 1 September 1955. Three years later, on 20 December 1958, Jennifer Aline came into our world. Both were born in San Francisco, though we were living in Corte Madera on the lower slopes of Mount Tamalpais in Marin County. Peter had his first birthday at Brown Gables in Seaford and made one or two other trips to England before going to school.

In our garden, Peter, Joyce & Bruce Taylor

Later, I did weekend teaching with the private 3R School, and unsuccessfully applied for exchange teaching, so decided to work full time for the 3R School. At about this time, Peter first attended a private school in San Francisco, then another in Corte Madera before finally going to state schools (called public schools in the US).

Fancying a change of direction, I tried my hand at life assurance sales with Lincoln National Life Insurance and later Sun Life of Canada for several years. In 1962, towards the end of this career of mine, Mum bought and moved to a house facing Big River Bay in Mendocino, California, so about every six weeks for the next 20 years we drove up to see her.

* * * *

In England it was called Guy Fawkes' Day. Part of what we used to chant on that day at St Pirans came to mind. "Remember, remember, the 5th of November."

To that I add: "I'll ever remember that on the 5th of November my beloved mother passed from this world to the next."

It was 1982. She was buried a few days later in the cemetery on the hill overlooking Mendocino and the Pacific Ocean, on the other side of which her husband's ashes are buried in the Yang Hwa Jin Seoul Foreigners' Cemetery, beside his father, with many other distinguished foreigners who aided Korea in the past.

Three years later her younger sister, Una Mouat-Biggs, who had a few years previously come from Mexico to live with her, died and was buried beside her.

17

Return To Teaching

I got back into substitute teaching in Marin County and finally taught full-time for two years in Lake County, California. It was here in Lake County, in 1964, that I had my son Peter in my science class, poor kid, right up front under his father's eagle eye! Meanwhile, Jennifer had started kindergarten.

One boy told me he was moving at the end of the term so he wouldn't have me again. I told him that another boy had said that when I was substituting in Marin County but the next Monday in another school he was in my class again. It was hard to escape from me!

And that was what happened to this boy, too! We both moved that year from Upper Lake to Windsor, and there he was in my fifth grade class, poor kid! I made him my 'special agent' to tell the class what I expected of them and what I would add in the way of interest when classes did as I told them. That changed his attitude.

I started a practice, developed from my insurance sales experience, of going to every single house of the children in my charge to meet the parents in their homes and tell them what I planned to do and what I expected their children to do. The result was a vast improvement on the part of my students and I made good friends too. Having started this in Upper Lake I continued it in Windsor. One former fifth grade student, now the captain of a huge container ship, still emails me from around the world.

At Upper Lake there was a lakeside party for the children at the end of the term. One boy said he would be absent that day, as parties were against his parents' religion. I said I was sorry that he would not be able to pass the end of term exam as this was a field trip and, following my usual rule, there would an exam on what we learned on the last day of school. I devised a test of things they were to find out during the party and he was able to come!

I taught my last 17 years in the Windsor School District, in Sonoma County, California, until I retired with 30 years of teaching in California state (public) schools.

I constantly sought better ways of teaching and finally found it in the Lozanov Method, also called Superlearning, the Accelerative or Accelerated Method, near the end of my career. The superintendent, surprised that so near retirement I should still seek better ways of teaching, granted me leave to attend a SALT conference (Society for Accelerative Learning and Teaching) during term time in Fort Collins, Colorado.

Over time I went to others in Texas, California, Florida and England. There, at St Mary's College of the University of London, I gave a talk at a SEAL conference (Society For Effective Affective Learning) and later even demonstrated the method in Australia.

But what finally hit the jackpot was a letter I wrote to the authors of the book *SuperLearning* – Sheila Ostrander and Lynn Schroeder – telling them of the success I had had with this method. I had used it just for spelling with the lowest of four fifth grade classes. Five months later the Stanford Achievement Test showed my low class a year ahead of the top class in that subject!

The authors asked if they could use my success in their advertising. I agreed and they advertised me in two more books, *Super-Memory* and *SuperLearning 2000*. I have received letters from teachers from every major continent as a result.

Later I joined various societies associated with the method in America, England, Australia and Japan. In time I dropped all save SEAL in England and went to several of their conferences over the years, eventually becoming their American representative until they ceased operation, I would think that due to the rising tide of the Internet enabling distant learning, this method would enhance world-wide education.

With the move to teaching in Windsor, we rented a house in an estate in Bennett Valley, Santa Rosa, so our children could attend schools there while we hunted for a permanent home. During our time there, Joyce and Jennifer went to England for quite a number of weeks into the school year. Jennifer had a glimpse of an English private school in Seaford and loved it.

Peter and I were on our own, he attending school in Santa Rosa and I teaching in Windsor. Breakfast was a bit of a rush as we were both in a hurry to get to our schools on time. The phrase 'haste makes waste' came true one day, when carrying an open jar of honey to the table I tripped and poured it into the drawer of knives and forks! There was a redoubled rush to clean that up as there would have been an ant invasion by late afternoon.

Long summer holidays had been built into teaching in America, based on the former need for children to help on the farm. The joker was in the low pay, but we had an English solution to that: Joyce's parents would pay for her and our children's fares once I was able to pay my own out of my Go to England savings account. Once it reached the return air fare – generally every three of four years – we would head to the land of our ancestors for the summer.

We spent other summer holidays camping in various state parks and Canadian provincial parks. In course of time our children went through high school and Peter went to Chico State College, graduating in Mass Communications. He then worked for small TV stations in Monterey and Santa Rosa, and finally for KGO, of the American Broadcasting Company, in San Francisco. He married and has a daughter.

Jennifer became a photographic model after completing a course in the subject, and went to Paris, then all over Europe, Africa, even the Indian Ocean and parts of the Caribbean and America. She met and married a famous French rugby player, Jean-Pierre Rives. They had houses in Paris and on the island of Ibiza in the Mediterranean, which we have visited.

As our children were on their own, our holiday horizons expanded to France, Spain and Ibiza, plus all the Hawaiian islands open to tourists, Alaska, Australia, New Zealand, the Western Isles of Scotland, Norway, the Shetland and Orkney Islands, and a canal cruise in England. Interspaced between these were trips to our favourite island of Kauai, in Hawaii. In 1993 we moved to Mum's former home, near Jennifer's. But we never thought of a return to Korea.

18

Father's Country

One Sunday in August 2005 our delightful interim priest, Father Leo, was absent from our Episcopal St Michaels and All Angels Church in Fort Bragg, so we became part-time Presbyterians at the local Mendocino Presbyterian Church instead. We had been there on various occasions so we hardly felt like visitors.

In the middle of the service the minister asked visitors to stand up and say where they were from. The man next to us stood up and said he was from Korea. When he sat down I told him we were both from Korea, too. Others in the church told me there was a Korean couple at Tote Fete, a delicatessen on Lansing Street, Mendocino. Talking to that couple I found they were also born in Seoul. I asked them if they would like to see a panoramic view of Seoul taken in 1924. They came to our house to see it and told the Korean consul in San Francisco about it. He asked if I would donate it to the Seoul History Museum.

I said I would send a copy, and at our daughter Jennifer's suggestion, included a copy of Mum's *Chain of Amber* asking if he knew a movie producer who might be interested in it. He did, and both he and the producer were amazed to find it contained a most important aspect of Korean history.

After a series of email exchanges, the producer, Stanley Kim, came from Seoul to Mendocino to see us, then turned the project over to friends of his at Indecom Cinema, a TV documentary film company in Seoul. They found records in Severance Hospital that matched those in *Chain of Amber* and realised the story fitted in with the most important South Korean celebration – National Independence Movement Day, on 1 March.

After many date changes by them and one last-minute health problem of mine in which our doctor suggested a few weeks' delay (I set that at two weeks), I said I would come.

* * * *

On Thursday 26 January 2006, Indecom Cinema's director, Jang Sang Il, and cameraman, Mr. Han, flew in from Seoul, picking up Chris Suh, an interpreter and California resident. That evening they arrived at the Pine Beach Inn, five miles north of Mendocino, then owned by Mr. Yun, from South Korea, whom I had met in the Presbyterian Church, thus starting the whole chain of events.

After dinner they came to The Haven, as Mum had called this house of ours, after the one we had had in Wonsan, North Korea, to tell us their filming plans for Friday. It was to be of ourselves, the house, Mum's grave in the cemetery and views of the town and the sea. After their explanation they returned to the inn saying they would return at 9am the following day.

Promptly at 9am they reappeared. After filming The Haven we drove up the hill opposite St Anthony's Catholic Church to Mum and Una's graves beneath the trees in the cemetery, with a view of the town and the Pacific Ocean stretching to the western horizon, beyond which my father is buried.

Here, we performed a Korean ceremony called the linking of the spirits. I was given a plastic bag containing earth from my father's distant grave on a hillside in the Land of the Morning Calm where I was born. I sprinkled the earth around my mother's last resting place. The Korean idea is that the earth around a grave contains the spirit of the dead, so earth from one grave sprinkled around the other grave re-unites their spirits in the afterlife.

Then we drove across Big River Bridge for the film crew to take views of the town and the sea beyond on a rather grey day. Saturday was spent filming views of The Haven, interviewing me and talking about my study of Hangul, the Korean phonetic script. Interviews with Joyce about her background in Korea followed.

The crew then went to Jennifer's barn and filmed her working on her art with a sound clip of my mother. Our free time was spent preparing for our departure.

* * * *

Sunday 29 January was another overcast day spent filming scenic shots, then some leaving and returning views. Returning home, we finished our packing and secured the house and car. At 5.30pm we all drove off to San Francisco airport, Joyce and I driven by Jennifer in her Mercedes. On the way we heard a gospel music station in Ukiah playing many familiar hymn tunes that brought to mind the Christian missions to Korea, which have wrought great changes in that land. All the way, the film crew were close behind us in their rental car.

Three and a half hours later, Jennifer brought us to the airport and the film crew led us to a place to sit down, took charge of our luggage and passports, bought our tickets and arranged for wheelchairs to take us to the departure lounge. In the meantime, Jennifer had gone to a park and fly and returned in their minibus so we could all sit down together for a meal.

When time came for check-in my titanium hip set off the alarm as usual, so of course I had to be individually checked. Then we were wheeled to the departure lounge for several hours of reading. Finally, at 12.30pm, we were wheeled to our seats next to the emergency exit on the Asiana plane, ahead of the other walk-on passengers. We left at 1am Monday morning and that's all we saw of that day. In 12 hours we arrived in Inchon on Tuesday.

Tuesday? What happened to *Monday*? In crossing the international date line, west to east, we had skipped a day.

Joyce and Jennifer managed very well with sleep during the 12-hour flight; I think I got about three hours, spending the waking hours watching the TV screens that gave the names of lands and islands we were passing over on the north circle route. Canada, the Aleutians Islands, Kamchatka (Russia), Hokaido and Honshu (Japan), then North and South Korea to land in the huge new Inchon airport.

The last time I came to Korea in 1937 it had taken me 14 *days* just to reach Japan from the Canadian west coast. Korea was several more days travel by train and ship.

After the usual interminable wait to go through customs and immigration we emerged to find that the super-efficient Indecom crew had loaded our luggage onto a minibus and were waiting to drive us through the city. We chose seats behind the driver and were introduced to another interpreter,

Gil, a lady who had spent some years in America. We drove out on the road to Seoul, where the traffic was hurtling down the freeway on the right. The surroundings looked more like southern California than the mountain-ringed land I remembered as Korea.

And then something occurred to me. Was I dreaming again? When I left Korea in 1940, traffic drove on the _left_, the way it does in Japan, which it had apparently learned from the British. No, this was indeed Korea, and I conjectured the change resulted from the American occupation after World War II, when the American Army would drive their vehicles on the right.

The land in that region of Inchon, having apparently been reclaimed from the mouth of the river Han, was flat and dull. Two hours driving finally brought our minibus to sights familiar to my memory of 66 years ago. There was the rounded dome of Seoul railway station and across the street I saw Nandaemun, the Great South Gate, which the Japanese had pronounced Nandaimon. It was one of the gates of the formerly entirely walled city.

A modern glass-fronted building stood in the place of the red-brick Severance Hospital where I was born 87 years before. I had returned to my home city, now ruled by its own people.

At 10.00am we arrived at the Frazier Suites, our home for the next nine days. After checking in we were whisked to the 20th floor, with a seemingly endless view of high-rise buildings that could have been in any Western city. Our apartment had two bedrooms and bathrooms, a sitting room and a fully equipped kitchen with washing machine. There was also a glassed-in porch outside the bedrooms. Very nice and modern.

Joyce and I lay down and slept for several hours. On waking we found Jennifer had ordered sandwiches for us, which we consumed with some delicious apples which were in the room when we arrived.

* * * *

At about 3pm the Indecom minibus picked us up and driving through the reborn city, whose population, which I guessed had been about a million when I left in 1940, had risen to over 10 times that number.

We ascended the formerly sacred hill of Namsan, the Japanese Shinto shrine above which no building was permitted to be built. The shrine and its worshippers had fled and the bus mounted ever higher up the zigzag road to the flat top where an open Korean pavilion stood.

To one side were some former fire-towers, used in past times for signalling. They had large openings low on one side and tall chimneys above to create a draft, evidently for starting fires from which flames or smoke would form the signals. On the other side of the mountain top was the base of a rotating tower, similar examples of which I have seen in Seattle and Canberra, with restaurants where diners can view the whole city as it appears to turn beneath them.

The Indecom crew led us to the tower, and Jennifer found a handy telescope which enabled her to see the mountains above our former home and the apartment buildings in front of Dilkusha, which she later used to find the house before I did.

We had a meal in the tower then the crew returned and drove us down town. Here, in what appeared to be the centre of the city, was a stream, numerous lit glass arches and Christmas trees on which people were attaching notes of the presents they would like as next year's Christmas presents.

These trees were put up for Christmas and kept until after New Year, thus covering holidays of different religions. Christians make up about 40 per cent of the population and the crosses of their churches are to be found in many parts of the city. We took photos and were filmed, then returned to our hotel.

The room was stiflingly hot and readjustment of the thermostat produced no relief, so we resorted to opening windows to the icy outside air. Later we found that there were hot water-filled pipes beneath the floor, doubtless an aid to comfort Koreans used to the super hot *ondal* floors in which flues from the kitchen fires ran beneath the floor. Far too hot for us, though!

On Wednesday, following a self-service breakfast in the dining room, we readied ourselves for Korea's cold February air and stopped in the lobby to ask the receptionist how to cool down the room. We were assured that it would be corrected by moving down a floor and they would have our belongings moved also.

Prompt as always, the ever helpful, considerate Indecom crew whisked us across the city, passing the Anglican cathedral, once so high on a hill, now dwarfed by the high-rise buildings all round it. We passed the former King's palace gate where flags flew and guards stood in their traditional colourful uniforms. It gave me a thrill to see a scene that perhaps my grandfather or father might have known before the Japanese seized the country.

High-rise buildings loomed above us all around, with giant TV screens advertising this and that, mostly in Hangul, but occasionally in Chinese characters. Rarer still, I could find characters I knew long ago when I studied Japanese and Chinese.

Eventually we came to a place that I recognised from the website of the Union Church which stands in the grounds of the Yang Hwa Jin Foreigners' Cemetery, once situated outside the city, above the river Han.

Now the city has encircled it. The minibus drove in and parked and we ascended the stone steps passing the church on the way to the last resting place of many distinguished foreigners. I saw a stone to Homer Hulbert, whose book *The Passing of Korea* is on my shelves with others about the country.

We came at last to Grandad's stone and before it one that I had had made for Dad. We noticed that a second stone plaque had been placed over the original, evidently after I had remarked that the first one implied that Dad had died twice without having been born! The first read: "d. Silver City, d. Glendale." It should have said: "b. Silver City"! This had been rectified on the new stone. Here we sprinkled the earth from Mum's tomb on Dad's, bowing in the Korean way as we did so. We took our own photographs and were filmed in the act. We placed flowers on each tomb and we returned to the minibus.

Joyce, Bruce & Jennifer Taylor beside A.W.Taylor's and his father's George Alexander Taylor, graves in the Yangwhajin Foreigner's Cemetery, Seoul, Korea, 2006

Just as the door was about to be closed, Pastor Prince of the Seoul Union Church arrived; he had been delayed attending to a sick child.

On return to the hotel we had a cooler suite on the 19th floor facing the mountains. Revelation! The views from our glassed-in porch were of the mountains I so longed for above my home! For over sixty years I had thought of them.

Below Pulpit Rock, North Mountain and others there were the ancient refurbished temples and palaces of old Korea. I was indeed home at long last! A saying from the Bible came to mind.

I will lift mine eyes unto the hills; from whence cometh my help? My help cometh even from the Lord, who hath made Heaven and Earth.

Psalm 121:1-2

* * * *

After lunch the Indecom crew drove us up beside the ancient
city wall and we walked along a path beside it, seeing the
ancient stones and above them new ones with cap stones on
the top. We were seeking Dilkusha, our family's Palace of
Heart's Delight.

I saw a point high up that looked as though it could be
the house, but just then the path came to an end and we
descended to the road below. Above some buildings was a
tall, wide tree. Could it be our ginkgo?

Jennifer led the way between two buildings and there it was!
Beyond it, Dilkusha. Its great garden had gone. A grove of
houses and apartments replaced the persimmon trees of
the past. Only the ginkgo tree still stood in that once huge
garden. Its fame had saved it.

The tree bore two plaques, one giving the address of the man
who cared for it and the other, cut in stone, its presumed
history. My former home now housed 17 families who had
fled the tyranny of North Korea. We went up to the house
and removed some plastic cans, laying bare the cornerstone
and its inscription: DILKUSHA 1923 Psalm 127 V.1. I
still recall the passage from the King James version of the
Bible:

Except the Lord build the house, they labour in vain that build it:
Except the Lord keep the city, the watchman waketh but in vain.

A Korean lady, the tenant of the rooms that had been
Dad's next to the ginkgo tree on the second floor, invited

us in. Leaving our shoes on the porch in the Korean way, we climbed the stairs in the hall and walked along a long, dark passage behind our former drawing room where we were greeted by the lady's husband at the entrance of Dad's former study-cum-bedroom.

They had lived there for 40 years after escaping from North Korea. We carried on a conversation through Gil, the Indecom interpreter, who had lived in Chicago for years and spoke good English.

The gentleman in the house had once worked for the US Army and had some knowledge of English. They offered us some fruit – some delicious apple and pear slices. We took photographs of the couple and said our goodbyes. The lady kindly helped me with my boots, we bowed to each other and walked to the ginkgo tree and its plaque.

The tree has a number of conflicting stories associated with it because of its long fame. Here, the plaque proclaimed that the tree had been planted by a General Kwon Yool (1537-1599), who was famous at the time of the Hideoyoshi invasion for holding off or defeating a superior Japanese force. This is a curious parallel with a story of one of Mum's ancestors: a young Cavalry officer in the Indian Army, who had been known as 'The Tiger With Spurs', had defended the original Dilkusha, in northern India, against a larger native force during the Indian Mutiny.

According to the late H H Underwood, a third generation Presbytarian minister of that family in Korea, there was evidence that the famous Admiral Soon Shin had been born on our Dilkusha property. Centuries before the American Civil War and the battle between the ironclads *Monitor* and *Merrimac*, Soon Shin had built 12 armoured warships which decimated an attacking Japanese fleet during the Hideoyoshi invasion. His 'turtle ships', covered with metal plates and spikes, defeated the Japanese manner of attack by boarding. The Korean ships were oar-propelled with a ram with which they sunk scores of enemy ships.

Some time in the 1920s or 30s, Kim Chusa, manager of W W Taylor & Co's curio shop, had found evidence of this ginkgo tree in a book published centuries ago. From this, Mr. Kim estimated the tree at that time to be about 600 years old. I suppose only a core drill could determine the real age of the tree.

Kim Chusa said that pine trees and ginkgos were always planted by temples or shrines. When the area next to the tree had been flattened to make an outdoor stage, an ancient stone altar was found, now covered by a wall-enclosed house, if it is there at all.

Our filming was finished and we walked down to the minibus. Just then Stanley Kim, the producer, drove up and invited us into his car. He drove us down to the King's palace and asked if we would like see it. Of course we would!

Parking the car in an underground garage we walked around the grounds. I took several photographs of the palace and its surroundings, including a giant incense urn. Then Stanley returned us to the hotel. During the drive I said I would like to see the premier of his new movie.

We had supper and soon went to bed where I pondered what I had seen. The glimpses of old Korea, surrounded by the abundant energy of the new, free South Korea – it filled me with exaltation to be even a part of this ancient-modern land in which I was born.

I felt grateful to my parents: to Dad for what he did, using the power of the Press to halt the Japanese atrocities which began on 1 March 1919; and to Mum, whose book brought attention to this part of Korean history, thus enabling our return. I wondered: "Can *I* do something for Korea?"

After breakfast on Thursday and preparations for departure we met the Indecom crew in the lobby and they whisked us off to a brand-new high-rise building, which viewed from above was seen to be shaped like a fish. It was the new Severance Hospital, revealing its Christian origin by using the religion's ancient secret symbol derived from the Greek word ichthys (fish) – an acronym for Iesous CHristos, THeou Yios, Soter (Jesus Christ, Son of God, Saviour).

The first missionary hospital of this Presbyterian Church was started by a single lady missionary doctor, who, acting as personal physician to Queen Min, was given a building for use as a hospital. It was replaced by the red-brick Severance Hospital in which I was born and which was destroyed in the Korean War.

Two missions combined – Yonsei University and Severance Hospital – to form the Yonsei Medical College and the 1,001-bed new Severance Hospital was born. It treats 8,000 outpatients daily and has a foreign section where people can an find English-speaking staff.

The minibus brought us to the rotating door of what looked like a fancy hotel, the inside resembling an airport. A lift (elevator) whisked us to the International Health Care Center where we met Dr John Linton, its director, who, like me, was born in Seoul.

As I had had a slight heart irregularity before we left for

Korea, Indecom wanted to be sure of my health. So I had an x-ray, an electrocardiogram and saw their top heart specialist, all the time accompanied by video and still photographers. To my relief I was declared okay.

Dylan Davis of the hospital's office of external affairs conducted us on a tour of the hospital facilities. We met Dr Chang Il Park, superintendent of the hospital, who presented each of us with an electric wrist watch bearing the Severance seal on its face.

Following that, we had lunch in one of the hospital's 14 restaurants. It was Japanese fare, but seeing Korea's national pickle, *kimchi*, I decided to try it for the first and last time! I then spent the rest of the meal stuffing things in my mouth to counteract the red hot pepper! Once is enough for me. Mum had had a similar reaction to *kimchi* many years earlier.

After a time in a rest area we were transported to the Underwood Memorial Statue in the grounds of Yonsei University, which had developed from the Chosen Christian College of our 1930s life in Korea. Here we met Peter Underwood, the fourth generation of his family in Korea, though he was a businessman unlike his forebears who were all Presbytarian ministers.

He showed us to their former family home, now a single-storey museum. When I had seen it last in 1937 it had two storeys. In the Korean War the North Korean Army used it as their headquarters and the US Air Force had bombed it. H H Underwood rebuilt it as a single storey after the war. It houses various mementos of the Underwood family's missionary life in Korea.

Next we went to the site of the former Severance Hospital, upon which now stands a tall, glass-fronted building. Here we met Professor Park, who had delved into the history of the hospital. He showed us a model of the old hospital and the houses behind it, where the doctors and their dependents lived.

I recalled a Christmas party among those houses, held by a lady called Mrs. Frampton. We talked to the professor about the activities on 1 March 1919 and my innocent part in it.

Later, I went out and noted how close this building was to the railway station, bringing to mind an event from my parents' day when a Korean had attempted to throw a bomb beneath the Japanese Governor-General's carriage. The bomb rolled on and injured by-standers. Dad and other foreigners rushed the injured to Severance Hospital just the other side of the road, as the Japanese police had had no idea what to do.

We returned to the hotel to spruce up, then were driven a few blocks to a Korean restaurant where we met Peter Underwood and his wife Diana, who acted as our hosts to a Korean meal. We enjoyed their company and mimicked Mum's reactions to *kimchi*, which she described in her book.

There was much less rice in the meal than in the past, rather little bits of many things and not much of anything. Neither Jennifer nor I thought much of Korean food – Chinese and Japanese food are still preferable to us.

I do recall one nice Korean meal – seaweed and rice at a temple in Kangwha, 66 years ago.

After dinner our hosts returned us to the hotel, where we soon retired to bed.

* * * *

Friday after breakfast I sat and read while Joyce and Jennifer walked around the nearby streets. On return they warned me of the cold weather outside, so I put on a double layer of clothes and took my super cold-weather jacket, which I called my suit of armour.

Jennifer went ahead to order a table in the dining room, we followed and got totally lost taking different lifts, never finding the way to our destination. Opening a door to a flight of stairs that she thought went up, Joyce fell down a flight *sans* banister or landing.

"Oh, my darling!" I gasped.

But she picked herself up and said she was all right. We went to the lobby and sat down, where she found she was bleeding in several places.

A young receptionist who had commandeered a first-aid kit was doing his best with sticking plasters (band aids) when both Jennifer and the Indecom crew appeared on the scene. They mutually decided that Severance Hospital was the place to go at once, though stoic British Joyce insisted she was fine, even though her boots were filled with her blood!

We piled into the minibus and returned to the hospital's International Health Center where Dr Linton took over and had a top skin specialist work on her. He decided she should stay in the hospital overnight at least and she got a nice room with a pleasant view.

Jennifer got all sorts of edibles for her so she wouldn't be dependent on Korean food.

The head nurse had stated that in the Korean fashion one of us had to stay with her. This was impossible as the documentary had to go on, but Dr Linton sorted the nurse out and as it was Dylan Davis, who had given us a tour earlier in the week, came in and spent several hours with her after we left.

His fiancée, whom he was to marry shortly, had other things to do that night. We found later that it was possible with resident nurses in the hotel to have someone to check up on Joyce in our suite during the day while the rest of us continued the work on the film.

The next stop for us was a Chinese restaurant on the other side of Seoul, whose roads seemed even more crowded these days, with cars travelling in four lanes each direction. Tae Yeong Kim, the CEO of Indecom Cinema, had invited us to dinner. He was partially paralysed from a fall he had had several years ago.

It was a private party for Indecom people in a restaurant belonging to a Chinese friend of his. Stanley Kim was there and following the meal Jennifer and I went to the premier of his thriller movie *The Vampire Cop*, which catered more to young adults and teenagers with a passion for thrillers.

It was well done and it was interesting to see the reactions of the audience, more like Americans than the Koreans I had seen 66 years ago under the iron fist of the Japanese military, when Koreans were second class citizens in their own land.

It was midnight by the time the show finished. Stanley

drove us back to the hotel and we quickly went to bed quite wiped out.

The hotel dining room was closed on weekends, so on Saturday Jennifer and I had breakfast at a cafe around the corner before the minibus took us to the hospital where Dr Linton said Joyce could stay until the evening.

So we went on to the Royal Palace. We got photos and films of the changing of the guard and viewed various parts of the palace area. Sundry questions were asked of me by the Indecom crew and my apparently quite eloquent answers were duly recorded.

We had a tour of the National Palace Museum conducted by its curator Park Sang-Kue, a delightful man who offered us some lovely gooey rice cakes from a refreshment stand inside. Continuing the tour, he kindly explained the various exhibits and, in passing, mentioned his desire to learn more English. I told him I could send him information that would help.

We returned to the hotel for lunch, then went to a Korean tea shop built in the traditional style in the 1930s. I had expected to sit on the floor in the customary Korean fashion of the days when the tea shop was built, but the room we were ushered into had chairs. Jennifer and I had different reactions – she thought it ancient and Korean, I thought it too modern and Western!

They played a recording of *Arirang*, a Korean folk song which Mum mentioned in *Chain of Amber* when she was in the Diamond Mountains with Dad. As we were leaving we were fortunate to see an early photo of the stream that ran through Seoul, later covered then revealed again recently by Mayor Lee Myung Bak. It is now quite a feature in beautifying the city.

Next we went to a series of curio shops, but in sharp contrast to the wealth of ancient artifacts we had had in the curio shop of W W Taylor & Co, there was little of interest to me, doubtless due to the devastation of the Korean War. There were some wooden cabinets and a few pairs of marriage ducks, which were given to young married couples as a symbol of fidelity, for these birds are said to keep one mate for life. But there was precious little else, so we returned to the hospital and brought Joyce home in the minivan.

Jennifer ordered some food and we had it in the room while we watched television for a while before retiring to bed early.

On Sunday Jennifer went to the nearby cafe and bought scones, jam, coffee and the like to eat in our rooms. The Indecom crew came at about 10am and Joyce was left with a lady helper.

We went to the Temple of Heaven in the former grounds of the Japanese Railways Chosen Hotel, now the huge Chosun Hotel across what was formerly Hasegawa-cho, where the Taylor building stood until the Korean War. The Korean name of the road portrays a princess who once lived in a nearby palace.

Jennifer, Gil and I obtained flowers from a stand outside and went into the temple grounds, placing the flowers on the altar. Then we walked round the circular building, taking photographs.

After admiring some stone drums outside the temple we

crossed the street to an empty lot where the Taylor building once stood. I suspect Bill Taylor sold the building after he left his job with the American Military Government and used the proceeds to set up his automotive business in Okinawa.

He kindly offered me a job after I was discharged from the Army, which I declined with thanks, as I had a more reliable Bill to provide me with four years of college education in order to become a teacher – a job then much in demand. This was the GI Bill, backed by law and far more reliable! So I was cut out of his will, which didn't surprise me, as I never expected anything from him anyway, as Dad and he rarely got on very well.

The Indecom Crew lead us to an Australian steak house for a good lunch, then we drove south a long, long way towards what had been the village of Jeam-ri in which, back in 1919, Dad had heard a massacre had taken place.

Having dispatched his brother Bill to Japan to cable Associated Press about the Korean Declaration of Independence before the imposition of censorship in Japan, Dad gathered the Rev H H Underwood and the American consul, Raymond Curtice as witnesses, drove to the village, gathered information and photographs of the carnage then on return took it to the Governor-General. He used the power of the Press to halt the massacre by informing the Governor that the US already knew of the declaration, and if the carnage did not stop the whole world would be informed of the Japanese atrocities.

We drove on a straight road with pine tree covered-hills scattered with Korean burial mounds here and there on the hills and eventually came to the Jeam-ri March 1 Movement Martyrdom Hall.

This was where the three witnesses mentioned above came in 1919. Shortly before, Korean Christians and possibly others had gathered before the local Methodist church and demonstrated for their freedom from Japan. The local police and a Japanese Army unit had rounded them up and told them they had an important message for them in the church. Locking them in, they set it on fire and shot the people inside. They also burned half the village down.

We entered the Memorial Hall and found an enlargement of one of the pictures Dad had taken of the despairing widows, and saw in the information three places where his name was specifically mentioned as having reported the incident to *The Japan Advertiser*, a newspaper in Japan.

We had a picture taken of Jennifer and I standing before Dad's picture of the widows. We also took photos of paintings of the freedom demonstration.

We met the church minister, the Rev Shin, for tea, then returned to Seoul, but too late to go to a folk village, where I had hoped that Jennifer might see the old Korean ways of life that I had known.

We returned to Joyce at the hotel and after a brief rest went to meet the president of the local Royal Asiatic Society, Sang Hyong Jang. Though I got his card and a photograph and had particularly wanted to talk to him, a tag-along reporter held the floor to the end. After they left we nibbled on some of the edibles brought back with Joyce from the hospital, then went to bed.

On Monday, Jennifer and I had breakfast in the dining room while Joyce had hers brought to her by a member of staff called Diana. The Indecom crew came to collect us with a wheelchair borrowed from the hotel for our trip to City Hall, a building retained from the days of the Japanese. We were taken into an inner room and seated behind a long table, with the Indecom and news photographers on the other side, photographing and filming us.

In due course the Mayor of Seoul, Lee Myung Bak, entered the room. (Incidently, Lee Myung Bak became President of South Korea in 2008.) We had a short private chat through his interpreter about my background in Korea, then I presented him with the 17 greatly improved and enlarged pictures from our family albums of Emperor Kojong's funeral, which had taken place on 3 March 1919 – two days after the Declaration of Independence from Japan had been publicly read, making 1 March Korea's most important holiday.

I also presented him with an equally improved and mounted panoramic photo of the one Dad had had taken of Seoul, probably in 1924, shortly after Dilkusha was first constructed. The picture's coverage extends from North Mountain to beyond South Mountain (Namsan) and includes Dilkusha, the 12-acre garden around it and the city wall just beyond it. In the foreground, the roof of one of the Methodist College buildings shows where my father and some missionaries were interned in World War II by the Japanese police.

My presentations being completed, the mayor placed a gold medal over my head, and presented me with a certificate in Korean and English stating that I was an honorary citizen of Seoul – of the same city in which I was born 87 years before.

I was also given a sample of granite mounted in a clear plastic paper-weight, the rock came from the stream the mayor ordered to be cleared to beautify the city. I now have a piece of South and North Korea, the latter being a large smoky quartz crystal from the Diamond Mountains which I picked up on my last trip to Korea over six decades ago.

At the end, people streamed from the room with Mayor Bak leading, wheeling Joyce in her wheelchair. Reaching the minibus, we were met by two men from City Hall who presented me with two framed photos of the presentation. One of them remarked that Koreans do things without delay these days. What a contrast to the days of Japanese misrule when it was tomorrow or the day after, probably never, that things were done.

Various newspapers came out with stories about us on that day.

The granite, the medal of my honorary citizenship in Seoul and its certificate are now on top of my bookcase along with the smoky quartz crystal.

We returned to the hotel for lunch then went off to the Methodist College where Dad had been interned for a few months at the start of World War II in the Pacific Ocean. Using her grandfather's telescope, Mum had been able to see him when they went out for exercise. The Methodists plan to make this old building into a museum.

We met a Korean Methodist Bishop who had been a student there in the days of Dad's internment.

Next we were taken to a spot on a steep hill which, by comparison of the mountain profiles, was thought to be the site of the 1924 panoramic photograph, a greatly improved copy of which I had given to the mayor. I subsequently received thanks from the Seoul Museum of History for it.

After a visit to the Yang Hwa Jin Cemetery for some parting shots and earth from Dad's grave to spread on Mum's Mendocino grave we returned to the hotel suite for supper with Joyce and early retirement.

We awoke to snow on Tuesday morning, so donning cold weather gear, Jennifer and I said goodbye to Joyce and left to meet the Indecom crew, who drove us to Peking Pass Road where the Independence Arch honours Korea's freedom from China. Beside it, Independence Park honours its freedom from Japan. We carefully trod the park's snow-covered paths, marvelling at the fairytale setting of the trees, with their branches highlighted with snow.

Coming finally to the Wall of the Fallen, we saw the names of many who bore the well-known name of Kim, which in the Chinese characters inscribed there is identical to the character for gold.

We photographed the scene, and were filmed there, standing in a valley of much Korean and personal history. The monument stands beside the road from which the Annual Tribute to China left on its long slow journey to Peking in the times when Korea, known as the Hermit Kingdom, was a vassal state of China. The road lies far below my favourite walk beside the ancient City Wall to Pulpit Rock.

We were then guided to the old Seidaimon prison to see the fiendish acts the Japanese authorities carried out on Koreans who dared the challenge their rule, other than killing them.

Returning for a final visit to Dilkusha, Jennifer and I walked to the far end of the house where my rooms had been, with Mum's on the second floor above them, and the paint storage room below. Beyond the house, where once there was a big dog run, there is now a huge apartment building.

Underneath our former home now there are a whole series of cubby-hole compartments built by poor escapees from North Korea. I felt glad that at least my former home provided them some succour from the tyranny of the North. What a pity such a rotten regime should have so beautiful a part of the country.

Stanley Kim, producer and president of Mythos Films of Seoul, who had got this whole idea of *Father's Country* going in the first place, had remarked that the house had been preserved because a subway train line ran beneath it. So the work of miners saved the house of a successful gold miner!

In addition, the background of General Kwon Yool and his association with the ginkgo tree, my father and possibly others who were great in the country's history, had caused the city government to contemplate turning Dilkusha into a historical monument.

We left Dilkusha for an excellent back-street pasta place. What a blessing to foreigners in Seoul, unused to eating *kimchi*! Fortunately, there are many eateries of various origins which do not require palates adjusted to the national pickle's high pepper content.

Following lunch we returned to the hotel to take Joyce to her appointment at Severance for a bandage change. Her wounds were already beginning to heal well.

At 7.30pm we were again picked up from the hotel and taken to a Chinese restaurant where Tae Yeong Kim, Indecom's chief executive, was treating the staff and ourselves. We were given a bag of the items we had lent them for use in the documentary and also some jade jewellery which an unidentified donor, a reader of *Chosun Ilbo*, a Korean daily paper, had left at City Hall for us. I later wrote to the paper to thank the mystery benefactor.

On Wednesday Joyce and I spent much of the day in the hotel suite. Jennifer had gone to an art showroom, owned by a friend of Tae Yeong Kim, to show them the catalogue of her art. We later heard that they wanted her to return in April and fill two floors with her collage works. She thought it would be lovely to return in the autumn when the colours of the Korean trees are at their best.

Our suitcases were packed so I went out to the porch every now and then to get a last glimpse of the mountains and temples of Korea. The next night we would be winging our way back to California. Our incredible journey to where I was born and where I first met Joyce, the delight of my life, would be over.

At about 6.30 in the evening Stanley Kim picked us up in his car and drove us to the Hyatt Regency hotel for dinner, then drove us home through much of the city, which made it hard to believe this was the Seoul we once knew.

Thursday – our last day! The day we make up for our missing Monday by having two Thursdays of 9 February, by virtue of crossing the international date line from east to west!

We went to breakfast in the dining room for the last time, returned to the suites then met in the lobby at 10.20am.

We were on our way to Joyce's former home, the British Embassy, which we had known in 1937 as the British Consulate General. The ambassador, Warwick Morris, had arranged for a car to deliver us there. It arrived on time and drove us to the embassy, passing the Anglican Cathedral on the way.

The Indecom people said they would return us to the airport at about 3pm, in the Korean fashion of saying farewell to departing guests.

What an utterly fabulous, totally changed land is the free country of South Korea today! When comes the time of total freedom for all members of the former Hermit Kingdom? When can the successful South extend its prosperity to its brothers and sisters in the North?

Would that I were in some position to do my bit towards the land of my birth. Is there a better way to teach English? Many Koreans are exposed to it in school, but few seem really to learn it.

Warwick and Pamela Morris came out of that familiar front door as we drove up and, as arranged, the Indecom crew were there to take some shots outside of the embassy, the grounds and ourselves with the Morrises. Entering the embassy, going first to the familiar morning room, well known to us both, brought back memories of Joyce's dear parents, then into the hall and upstairs where Joyce found her former bedroom above the front door. Returning to the morning room we sat and talked with the Morrises while having coffee and cakes. It brought back a flood of memories of the Korea we had known 66 years before.

The Morris's home in England is in Tunbridge Wells, Kent,

the next county to Sussex where Joyce's parents had retired. They were a really delightful couple, so very English. It would be a joy to meet them again.

We went out to more Indecom pictures, then back to the car and thus to the hotel.

After lunch we returned to our rooms for one last look at the mountains above Dilkusha and the ginkgo tree. Then in the hotel lobby we found that Stanley Kim had brought his car to drive to us to the airport. On the way, we were rewarded with a final glimpse of Dilkusha from the road.

During the drive I told Stanley of the success I had had in teaching and in helping other teachers around the world with improved methods. I wondered aloud whether there was a way of extending that to Korea?

Mr Jang and Mr Han followed in another car to assist our departure and get some more film at the airport, which was shrouded in fog, then got us wheelchairs and booked our seats on the plane by the bulkhead.

We left at about 7.40pm and 12 hours later Asiana Airlines had delivered us to San Francisco where we met our son Peter, who loaded our luggage into Jennifer's car.

Heading north we crossed the Golden Gate Bridge, and north of Cloverdale we turned onto the country road that leads to the coast and our home in Mendocino.

In less than a fortnight the story of the Taylor family in Asia had been concluded, its last member made an honorary citizen of Seoul by the then Mayor Lee Myung Bak, now President of South Korea.

Koreans have learned from the resulting documentary, *Father's Country*, that they did have Western helpers when they strove for freedom on 1 March 1919.

Glossary

Note:-- Considerably more can be found out about many of these notes by adding the country of origin and accessing GOOGLE with a computer.

Korean [K] Japanese [J]

Accelerated Learning
The following books greatly expanded my use of the method also known as Accelerative Learning, SuperLearning, the Lozanov Method and Suggestology):
Accelerated Learning by Colin Rose
Details on this book can be found at www.accelerated-learning-uk.co.uk
Accelerated Learning for the 21st Century:
The Six Step Plan to Unlock Your Master Mind (1997)
Book by Colin Rose & Malcolm J Nicholl. Published by Delacorte Press, Bantam Doubleday, Dell Publishing Group,1540 Broadway, New York, NY 10036.

Ahma
Korean nurse-maid.

Anglican Cathedral
in Seoul, Korea, http://www.skh.or.kr/

Assay Office
Where chemical tests determined the mineral content and quantity in rock samples and the relative yield per ton, of gold, silver, lead and other metals.

Atabrin
An anti-malarial drug used by the US Army in World War II in the South Pacific to combat malaria.

British Embassy Seoul Korea
During Japanese rule, 1910-45, the British Embassy was called the British Consulate General (G H Phipps, Consul-General (in the 1930's until Japan declared war in 1941).It now has a website:- http://ukinkorea.fco.gov.uk/en

Busan or Pusan[K] Fusan)[J]
The nearest Korean port to Japan in the south-east of Korea.

Chain of Amber
Autobiography by Mary Linley Taylor. Copies are still available. from:-

Gallery Bookshop.
PO Box 270
Main & Kasten Streets, Mendocino, CA 95460 U.S.A
707-937-BOOK (2665) FAX707-937-3737
Web page:-gallerybooks.com
E-mail:-info@gallery bookshop.com

Chosun Ilbo
A Korean language daily paper, in Seoul, Korea.

Colonial status
Following the Russo-Japanese War Japan started taking control of Korea and in 1910 Korea was declared a Japanese province. At that time its territory stretched from the Yalu river to the Korea Strait, including the island of Cheju-Do.

This colonial status lasted until 1945 with the end of World War II.

Diamond Mountains Kumgangsan[K] Kongosan[J]
Mountains named after the Diamond Sutra of Buddhism on the East coast of North Korea.

Dilkusha
"The Palace of Heart's Delight". The Taylor family home in Seoul named after a palace my mother saw in Lucknow, India, on her honeymoon. General Kwon Yool is said to have planted the ginkgo tree in Dilkusha's garden. He defeated a superior Japanese force during the Hideyoshi invasion (1592-8). There is a plaque to that effect on the tree, which I saw in February, 2006.

Early Christian Fish Symbol =Isous Christos Theou Yios Soter = ichthys = Greek for 'fish'
The New Severance Hospital in Seoul is in the shape of this early Christian fish symbol.

English Public Schools
These and the Preparatory schools are fee-supported private schools. Also called independent schools.

Futon
A flat, 5cm-thick mattress with fabric exterior stuffed with cotton batting which makes up a Japanese bed.

Forty Li of Shining Sands
12-mile Wonsan Beach on north-east coast of Korea, just south of Wonsan which is now a North Korean naval base. It was called Gensan by the Japanese during their rule of the whole of Korea (1910-1945).

Galena
Lead sulphide (grey-black in colour).

Hangul
Korean phonetic alphabet developed in 1443 by King Sejong, it is said to be one of the world's finest orthographic systems.

Hermit Kingdom
A name used for Korea as for centuries the country excluded foreigners.

Indecom Cinema
Makers of the TV documentary Father's Country (2006) CEO: Tae Yeong Kim. Director: Sang Il Jang.
Producer Ik San Kim, 122-1, 3F Yonggang-Dong, Mapo-Gu, Seoul 121-876, Korea Tel: 822-711-3890-2; fax: 822-706-3302 HP: 32-11-396-387 Email: nomads21@hanmail.net

Isthmus of Panama
A narrow section of land between Panama City and Colon in Panama, through which the Panama Canal runs, connecting the Pacific to the Atlantic Ocean. Panama lies between Costa Rica to the north and Colombia to the south.

Japanese Baths
Japanese baths were wooden tubs with built-in stoves: water was poured into the tub and a lid was put in place; a fire was lit and kept going for about two hours, producing a nice hot bath to soak in after having washed and rinsed off outside the tub.

Kim, Stanley (Ik San Kim)
Producer and President of Mythos Films, who initiated the idea of "Father's Country." Mythos Films, 2F, 656-19,

Yuk Sam-Dong, Kang nam-ku, Seoul, Korea 135-913. Tel: 82-2-568-8210; fax: 82-2-568-8419; mobile: 82-11-9955-3235. Email: kimbrick@naver.com

Kojong, King
Korean Emperor known as The Lord of a Thousand Isles (there are in fact more than 3,000 islands off Korea's coasts)

Korea
Some of Korea's ideas were centuries ahead of other countries, including an astronomical observatory built in 634 AD, movable metal type developed two centuries ahead of Europe and armoured warships sent into battle in the 16th century. Rain gauges, sun dials and water clocks were also independently developed.

Korean automatic rice mill
Rice, poured into the hollowed end of a vertical tree trunk set low in the ground, was pounded by a wooden hammer attached to a horizontal beam, pivoted so that water pouring into the opposite spoon-shaped end tilted it down and emptied it, causing the hammer end to fall and pound the rice.

Korean Declaration of Independence proclaimed
1 March 1919, when the Koreans declared independence from Japan. This date became the most important South Korean national holiday, called National Independence Movement Day.

Li
Korean measure of distance: one third of a mile.

Lyme Regis
Town in Dorset, UK, home to Liassic rocks of the Lower Jurassic period,190 million years old. I found an ammonite about 30cm in diameter and part of the jaw and teeth of an itchyosaur, among others, 72 years ago on this beach.

Menzies, Commander Gavin Royal Navy (rtd)
Author of 1421: The Year China Discovered the World (2002); and 1421The Year that China Discovered America (2003) 1434 The Year A Magnificent Chinese Fleet Sailed To Italy And Ignited The Renaissance (2008) See also:- www.1421.tv

Mudong
A female witch doctor. Mudong means 'deceiving crowd'[K], which just about sums up the quality of this 'medical' practice.

Namdo
The name of our bright male Korean cook.

Nandaemun [K] Nandaimon [J]
The Great South Gate of Seoul.

Oriental Consolidated Mining Company (OCM)
Company in Pyeongonbuk-do, the northern province of Korea – American skill and machinery combined with King Kojong's mines.

Ondal or Kahn Floor
Under-floor heating by the smoke from the low kitchen stoves flowing through stone passages under the floor of Korean houses.

Pack Rat
Pack rats are found in deserts and highlands in the western

United States,northern Mexico and western Canada. They
build nests of twigs called middens in caves, attics and walls
of houses. People who hoard things are often called pack
rats.

President Woodrow Wilson
In January 1918 President Wilson spoke of the right of self-
rule for small nations in a speech to the League of Nations.
Hearing of it, Korean patriots were inspired to issue their
Declaration of Independence from Japan.

Robin Hood's Bay
Bay in Yorkshire, UK, home to 190 million year-old
Liassic rocks, of the Lower Jurassic period; ammonites and
belemnite fossils found there in large quantities.

Royal Asiatic Society
Sang Hyong Jang President CPO Box 255 Seoul Korea
Tel: +82-2-763 9483 Fax: +82-2-766 3796 (As of 2006)

Shoji screens
In Japanese architecture, this is a room divider or door of a
wood frame covered with rice paper.

Sprue
A wasting tropical disease.

Staithes
Town on the Yorkshire, coast UK, where Liassic rocks from
the Lower Jurassic period,190 million years old, can be
found. Many fossils to be found there also.

St Pirans-on-the-Hill
This prep school in Maidenhead, Berkshire, UK, formerly
a boys'school but now co-educational, still exists today. The

school was named after an Irish saint who built his church on the sands of what is now Perrenporth, Cornwall. School website: www.stpirans.co.uk

SuperLearning (1979)

by Sheila Ostrander and Lynn Schroeder with NancyOstrander. Delta/The Confucian Press. A Delta book published by Dell Publishing,1 Dag Hammarskjold Plaza, New York, NY 10017. This book afforded me great success in this teaching method.

The following two books mention my success with the method and my simplified version of it called AIM (Accelerative Introductory Method).

Further information about these books is available on the authors' web site: www.superlearning.com

SuperMemory: The Revolution (1991)

by Sheila Ostrander and Llynn Schroeder. Published by Carroll & Graf Publishers, 260 Fifth Avenue, New York, NY 10001.

SuperLearning 2000

by Sheila Ostrander and Llynn Schroeder with Nancy Ostrander.Published by Delacorte Press,Bantam Doubleday. Dell Publishing Group,1540 Broadway, New York, NY 10036

Tangye hot bulb gas fired engines driving lathes in the gas lighted St Pirans School machine shop. Years after leaving school I saw a similiar engine in a museum in Matakohe, North Island, New Zealand. They were evidently widely used before the invention of electrical ignition..

Tatami Woven straw mats used on the floors of Japanese houses

Tributers' tunnels

The miners of these tunnels paid a portion of what they mined to the Company for the right to mine the rest, like sharecroppers.

Turtle ships
Metal covered ships with spikes on top to discourage boarders. The Turtle ships of Korean Admiral Soon Shin decimated a larger Japanese armada in 1592.

Union Church (of Seoul)
E-mail:- pastor@seoulunionchurch.org
144 Hapchung-dong, Mapo-ku Seoul, 121-885 Korea
This is along side the Yang Hwa Jin Foreigner's Cemetery.

Yangban
An upper class Korean official, of the former Korean Empire.

Yang Hwa Jin Foreigner's Cemetery
Cemetery next to Union Church, Seoul, Korea. (See address above)

Acknowledgements

<u>For Expert Assistance, my thanks to</u>:-
Editor Julie-Ann Amos, and Associates.,
www.exquisitewriting.com

Brett Flanigan personal family photographs.
In the cover, illustrations and language this book follows
the ways of "Chain of Amber" by Mary Linley Taylor, my
mother's autobiography of her life in Korea between World
War I & II, Published in England a decade after her death
by :- The Book Guild, 25 High St. Lewes, Sussex,
England. (c) Mary Linley Taylor 1991.

For my unusual life in Korea, America and England I have
my remarkable American father, Bruce, known also as
"A.W" and my wonderful, adventurous English mother,
Mary, to thank.

Mary's best friends Aline Phipps and her husband Gerald,
British Consul General in Seoul, for a second time, from
1935 to 1942 and their daughter Joyce who in due course
married me and transformed my life.

My thanks to our family members for all their kind
assistance. To my wonderful patient wife, Joyce, whose
background in Asia and England is akin to my own, for
her constant cheerful encouragement which enabled the
completion of this book.

To our son Peter for his patient repeated instructions on how to overcome the mysterious ways of computers and associated gear!

To our daughter Jennifer for her artistic talent which greatly enhanced the make up of the book's cover design and selection of it's photographs. She suggested asking the Korean Consul if my mother's *Chain of Amber* would interest a Korean movie producer: one did, and Stanley Kim, producer and President of Mythos Films of Seoul, Korea, who came to see us and contacted his friends in Indecom Cinema of Seoul, resulting in the TV documentary *"Father's Country,"* shown on Prime Time on South Korean National Television. This was on National Independence Movement Day, March 1st 2006, their most important holiday.

Supplemental
Illustrations

Author, Bruce Tickell Taylor

The Taylor Family Top, left to right:-
Peter, Bruce, bottom left right:-Jennifer & Joyce Taylor

Clockwise figures around Korea map, Albert Wilder Taylor & Mary Linley
Taylor, Bruce Tickell Taylor & Dilkusha by the Ginkgo Tree.

I was a miner, soldier, sailor, rich man, poor man, teacher.
These are my recollections of the end of two empires –
the Japanese and the British – of growing up in Korea,
America and England, of visits to 40 other lands and
of making myself understood in 10 languages.

Presentation of Honorary Seoul Citizenship to the Author by Seoul Mayor
on February 2nd, 2006. left to right :- Joyce Phipps Taylor,Bruce Tickell
Taylor,Mayor Lee Myung Bak,Jennifer Aline Taylor. In 2008 Mayor Lee
Myung Bak, became South Korea's President.

About the Author

Born in Korea shared his bed with Korean Declaration of Independence. Private American, British, education, 9 years in Korea, college in California, 4 years Regular Army. 30 years California teaching. Global "Superlearning" success. Acted in *Father's Country* " TV Historical Documentary. Granted Honorary Seoul citizenship by Mayor, now South Korean President. as of 2008